Festivals
Together

Creating all-age worship through the year

SANDRA MILLAR

First published in Great Britain in 2012

Society for Promoting Christian Knowledge
36 Causton Street
London SW1P 4ST
www.spckpublishing.co.uk

British Library Cataloguing-in-Publication Data
A catalogue record for this book is available from the British Library

ISBN 978–0–281–06631–5
eBook ISBN 978–0–281–06632–2

1 3 5 7 9 10 8 6 4 2

Typeset by Graphicraft Limited, Hong Kong
Printed in Great Britain by Ashford Colour Press

eBook by Graphicraft Limited, Hong Kong

Produced on paper from sustainable forests

Also available:
Worship Together: Creating all-age services that work

Contents

Part 1
Creating all-age worship: the key components

Part 2
The service outlines

With thanks to all those churches willing to take risks and create worship for whoever is present

Part 1

Creating all-age worship: the key components

Before the beginning

If you have already used *Worship Together*, then you might want to skip this chapter, which gives a brief overview of some of the ideas and principles that underlie the worship outlines provided.

The worship outlines in this book are designed for all kinds of churches, big or small, well-resourced or not. Mostly they do not require endless cutting-out, hours creating complex visuals or developing demanding dramas that will only work with a large congregation. They do not assume that there is a worship band or a well-resourced and trained team of leaders (though worship bands are great and training is invaluable!). They don't even assume that you will have lots of children and young people present. What they do offer is an approach that will work for whoever is present, with creative ways of hearing God's story that open up the possibility of encounter with his love.

Introduction

Festival is a great word and a great experience, one deeply embedded in contemporary culture.

It is estimated that there are at least five hundred music festivals alone each year in the UK, plus countless other types. There are history festivals, literary festivals, cricket festivals – almost any summer event can have the word 'festival' added to create an expectation of a time to relax, enjoy, be with family and friends, and perhaps discover something new. There are a few that are specifically for children, but all of them include elements that are for children and families, and in many cases children are simply there, taking part and sharing in the day.

At a music festival, I watched a three-year-old sitting high on his dad's shoulders, swaying to the rhythm and clapping enthusiastically as a well-known indie band performed on stage. Elsewhere in the crowd I saw a very mixed group, ages ranging from around eight to fifty-plus, including teenagers, laughing and dancing together. A festival is truly an event for everyone, an event for all the family.

A festival is truly an event for everyone, an event for all the family

It's not so very long since it was the Church that provided this kind of occasion, when all ages celebrated together. There were days when statues were carried, crosses were moved, banners were paraded, girls and boys dressed up and the holy day began with worship and movement before becoming a holiday for everyone. The early twentieth-century author Elizabeth Goudge includes wonderful moments of church festivals in several of her books, such as *A City of Bells* and in her famous children's classic, *The Little White Horse* (sadly completely omitted in the film version, *Moonacre*):

> The church was full of sunshine, children, and music . . . Robin gave him the great cross-handled sword and, holding it aloft like a processional cross, Old Parson went striding down the aisle with it and out into the sunshine . . . When they were nearly at the summit Old Parson made them stop and get their breath back, and then, singing once again, they made their way beneath the branches of the beech-trees and through the doorway in the broken wall and into the paved court beyond . . .
>
> First, standing before the altar . . . he said a very long prayer . . . for forgiveness . . . And then he prayed that for ever and ever this place should now be a holy place, and that no wickedness should be done here any more . . . And then Robin took his shepherd's pipe . . . and to its accompaniment they sang . . . all the praising things they could think of. And then at last, reluctantly, because it was so lovely up here on the hill, they turned themselves about and went in procession back to the village, singing all the way.[1]

You really have to read all of chapter 9 in *The Little White Horse* to get a full sense of the joyful festival that takes place when Paradise Hill is given back to God. It has procession and song and stillness and excitement – all the elements of a good festival. But somehow it seems so much more difficult to do this in our contemporary church world. There are still Whit Walks in many northern towns, including the city of Manchester as well as smaller places. But a quick search on the Internet will show that they are not quite as much of a public event as they used to be, although they still retain a real sense of festival. There are still wonderful pilgrimage events, when people of all ages gather from across a diocese or region and come together to celebrate the life of a local saint.

Only recently I listened to a young person reminiscing about Bank Holiday Mondays spent walking with family and friends before joining in worship at the local cathedral. A few years ago the Church tried to capture this sense of carnival when lots of Christians took to the streets to 'March for

Jesus', accompanied by drums, clowns, balloons and song.

In other parts of the world, and in other faiths, colour and movement are an integral part of religious life. Festivals almost always involve some kind of public procession, accompanied by crowds, whether moving in sadness or joy. A friend recently visited Sri Lanka, and described the extraordinary festival of Kandy Perahera, a solemn Buddhist tradition. As the procession moved through the streets, those working in shops or chatting in cafés simply stopped and stood for a moment as it went by. The festival has an impact on society as well as on those taking part, yet our Christian milestones seem to have become private affairs, in spite of their huge importance.

The difference between the kind of festivals now flourishing in society and those outlined in Scripture and handed down in the tradition of the Church is that our festivals are a re-enactment of sacred stories. Christian festivals are not about entertainment (although there may well be lots of fun and laughter), nor even about education (though we may be discovering new things about God's involvement with the world). Sometimes they will be joyful occasions, at other times they will involve recalling moments of pain and failure, but whatever the theme the intention is that everyone will be involved. They allow us an opportunity to enter into the events that stand at the heart of our history and our faith and help create a space in which people of all ages have the possibility of encountering God.

> **Christian festivals are not about entertainment (although there may well be lots of fun and laughter), nor even about education (though we may be discovering new things about God's involvement with the world)**

Worship with whoever is present

Festivals are genuinely worship for all ages or, as I often call it these days, worship for whoever is present. It is not dependent on the presence of children to make it happen, but will truly have the potential to allow everyone from nought to one hundred the possibility of worship and encounter. Yet there seems to be something strangely paralysing about the words 'all age' to our churches, with its understood subtext of 'Oh my goodness, that means there will be children there! What are we going to do?' Yet week in, week out, year in, year out, the Church holds worship that engages a wide range of different needs and life experiences, without anyone getting too worked up about it. We don't worry about a congregation with some young professionals in their thirties (for some of us that would be positively exciting!) alongside the residents from a local care home plus the regulars who are between 65 and 90 years old. Somehow we trust the words of worship, the Scriptures and the prayers to connect with life. All our worship is for all ages: children are simply part of the mix. There may be occasions when we want to have special events for them or reflect on things that are clearly adult, but our festivals should be for everyone.

> **All our worship is for all ages: children are simply part of the mix. There may be occasions when we want to have special events for them or reflect on things that are clearly adult, but our festivals should be for everyone**

The Hebrew Scriptures lay down guidelines for the commemoration of significant events in Jewish history, and it is clear throughout that there is a great deal of drama and participation by the people. The festival of booths (Leviticus 23.42; Nehemiah 8.13–18) always sounds like a great occasion, with people working together to build huts out of branches, then camping in them for a week, before holding the solemn assembly. The festival of Purim, which recounts the story of Esther, is also a marvellous occasion for family involvement, with much cheering and laughing throughout. However, it is not just the happy times which are 'for the children'. There are occasions when the people of God are called together for moments of high solemnity, such as the dedication of the temple or to be called to account for all that has gone wrong: 'Blow the trumpet in Zion; sanctify a fast; call a solemn assembly; gather the people. Sanctify the congregation; assemble the aged; gather the children, even infants at the breast' (Joel 2.15–16).

The Christian calendar likewise gives lots of opportunities to engage experientially with the story of the faith, at moments of celebration and also at moments of solemnity. Some of our festivals overlap with a festival in popular culture, most notably Christmas, and churches will use these occasions to engage not only with the regular congregation but also with those on the fringes of church life – and that will often mean younger adults and children. The challenge is to make the festival in the church significant and memorable for those who attend. It does not need to be memorable because it is better or brighter than the events going on in the secular world. It needs to be memorable because we have created a space in which all those present have the opportunity of encounter with God and of discovering a sense of belonging, together with a chance to experience the ways in which the story of God and God's people still touches our lives today.

'Encounter' and 'experience' are the key words. Being present and entering into an event is very different from being told or taught about it. That's

> **Being present and entering into an event is very different from being told or taught about it**

why people go and queue for hours on the Mall to see great royal occasions. We know we will get a better view on television, but there is something indescribably different about being there. Being able to experience the atmosphere is why families take toddlers to rugby football or soccer or a live play: they want them to catch hold of something beyond words. The story is caught, not taught.

A couple of years ago I was present in a cathedral at a special event for children. The highlight was a performance by a mime artist, who presented the story of Peter's life. The children were clearly entranced as the story (told by a narrator on CD) and movement worked together to convey Peter's despair at failing Jesus. Then came an amazing moment, when the music changed, and the mime artist made a huge leap into the air as 'Peter' realized that Jesus was alive again. Four boys, sitting near the back, leapt from their seats and punched the air, crying 'Yeah!' before realizing where they were, and

sheepishly sliding back into their seats. These boys had truly experienced the story, perhaps for the first time in their lives.

The shape of the Church's year

The church year takes us through the whole story of our faith in a series of festivals. We begin in the waiting time of Advent, looking forward to the coming of Christ. We move to the joyous celebration and mystery of the incarnation, the revealing of Christ to the world through the visit of the Magi and the response of Simeon, celebrated at Candlemas. At the centre of the church year is the great, intense, demanding series of events that lead us through Holy Week to Easter, stories with immense drama and emotion. We celebrate the coming of the Spirit to the Church, the generosity of God in Harvest and then remember his faithfulness through generations in the stories of saints. Alongside these there are other traditions related to the story of our lives – Mothering Sunday, Remembrance Sunday as well as local events. The opportunity to be part of these occasions is about being present, about being there rather than learning about it from others.

This is why festivals matter to us in the Church. Those present have an opportunity to catch something significant, which may be beyond words, but will be made up of the kind of movement, stillness and sounds that are characteristic of festivals everywhere. Unfortunately we seem to have developed an idea in the Church that some things are 'good for children' and some are not, so we may well have thought carefully about how to make our Christmas services engaging, yet never thought about Maundy Thursday as an evening for families. The whole cycle of the church year allows us to discover the stories that lie at the heart of our faith, and rediscover their relevance as we return to them at the different stages of our own lives.

Planning all-age worship that works: the key components

The challenge is how to make festivals, whether joyful or solemn, into these kinds of all-age experiences. Good all-age communication happens throughout our culture, and sometimes it seems as if the Church has handed over this task to these other agencies. Yet by looking carefully at these activities, noticing the way things happen, and then building some of those ideas into our worship, then we too can recreate festivals that truly engage all ages (there is much more on doing this in *Worship Together*). There are five key factors that help to create effective all-age communication, and these factors are also vital in creating all-age festivals that work. The five key elements are passion, structure, multi-sensory experience, mystery and universal themes. The rest of this chapter explains each of these briefly.

Passion

Before the ideas, before the music and the words, there is one crucial thing that festivals that work for all ages have in common. The more I have talked to people about all-age worship, and the more I have observed events in our culture, the more I have realized that this has to underlie the content of any event, whether secular festival or Christian celebration.

The central ingredient, the key to successful all-age events, is as simple as passion. And alongside a passionate excitement there is an unmitigated enthusiastic expectation that children of all ages want to be there. As a family make their way through the site of a well-known music festival, Dad is waxing lyrical about all that is happening. He is pointing out interesting things in the crowd, talking about what they will see later on: and the passion of adults is contagious. Passion is not simply about an extrovert zest for life. It can equally be a quiet, deeply held conviction that something really, really

> **Passion is not simply about an extrovert zest for life. It can equally be a quiet, deeply held conviction that something really, really matters**

matters. Some children develop interests because of particular teachers or clubs, but many more have life-long interests because of their parents. Yet all too often adults approach the idea of children and church with the opposite of enthusiasm: 'I know it won't be very good, but don't worry because if you don't like it you can go to the back corner and do some colouring.'

Do colouring when the most amazing story in the world is unfolding in front of you? Why are we not jumping up and down with excitement and anticipation at the prospect of introducing our children to these stories? When this passion is in place, then a willingness to be imaginative grows, and it is from this passion that an ability to tell the story in a mind-catching way can also flourish. For churches, this kind of enthusiastic expectation that people of all ages will want to be engaged in our festivals and special occasions has to be part of the mindset of the congregation. It may begin with one of the leaders, but it is also the responsibility of the whole people of God to share eagerly the great stories of their faith. Although this kind of expectation is vital, by itself it is not enough. There are some other factors which help to make all-age communication happen.

Structure, pattern and repetition

One of the most important aspects of creating events that work for everyone is structure, alongside pattern and repetition. Some church worship has a weekly pattern and repetition, but at other times the pattern is rehearsed on an annual cycle. For example, in the Church of England, we use different responses from those used in the rest of the year during the

> **Structure, alongside pattern and repetition, is used by successful all-age events in the media and in our culture**

Easter season (from Easter Eve until Pentecost), though it is the same response for those weeks, and the same response each year. This kind of pattern is vital in building a sense of familiarity and belonging. This is how we enter inside the story, rather than having to spend too long worrying about where we are, and whether we know what is about to happen. A familiar opening allows us to relax into the event, thus freeing our spirits to encounter God, rather than letting minds and emotions worry anxiously about whether the right thing is happening. This is the technique used by successful all-age events in the media and in our culture – whether it is the use of a theme tune or an opening catchphrase, or in a physical environment, making sure that the welcome at every Disney Park is the same!

The difficulty for us in church is ensuring that there is enough that is familiar to those who attend infrequently, while still picking up the themes and resonances of the particular festival. A new approach is only new to those who are already familiar with what is happening; for others the whole event may be new. It can be easier to introduce completely new approaches when everyone is wrong-footed together – and to be wrong-footed we need to know what the right-footed approach feels like. For those with a residual memory of church, or a regular but infrequent attendance (e.g. every crib service), it will be the basic framework or structure that gives the sense of confidence and familiarity. Within that framework many different things might happen, but the walls are always in the same place.

Service structure

The good news is that worship has the same basic structure, whether it is for an ordinary Sunday or for a festival. The basic shape is as follows.

WE GATHER

This might be as simple as the opening responses or as complex as an activity involving a procession, drama and music. A significant part of gathering is usually a time of confession and absolution – we say sorry. This is an important moment in worship, as it allows for reflection on our lives and also on the failures we encounter in our world. It is also a reminder of the central message of our faith – the wonderful good news of God's love reaching out to us through Jesus.

WE LISTEN

There is a point in every act of worship where we listen to God's word, read from Scripture and let the word connect with our lives as either we explore it together or reflect together through a talk, activity or sermon. The word can be presented in all kinds of imaginative and engaging ways, in the reading of Scripture and in exploring together how that word touches our lives.

WE RESPOND

Having heard the word of God, we need time and space to allow ourselves to respond, whether in prayer for ourselves or for the world, and to allow ourselves another opportunity to be multi-sensory,

for physical and imaginative movement. Part of our response is also sharing in bread and wine – although strictly speaking the word Eucharist also refers to the whole liturgy.

WE GO OUT

Endings are as important as beginnings, and the final part of our worship needs to turn attention towards living our faith in our daily lives.

In some of the festival services this basic shape becomes more noticeably flexible. There is a repetition of the central pattern of listening and responding, as we may listen to more than one reading with more than one theme. This may all take place within the shape of a procession or even a meal, as the shape is also the vehicle for engaging with the story. However, it is also important that the structure of each individual occasion becomes familiar over the years, with the changes that happen occurring slowly to ensure that the worship remains alive and relevant. This is the way that successful products continue not just for a few years, but last for generations. A visit to a 'bygones' museum serves as a reminder of how subtly household names change their packaging and image over the years. A name like 'Fairy' or 'Mars' maintains a strong identity so that people continue to trust the product, and yet there are also tiny incremental shifts in design and style so that it is only when the 1950s product is placed next to the 2010 product that we see how dramatic the shift has been. In the Church, we often struggle to make small changes, and then make giant leaps all at once, leaving people feeling that nothing is recognizable, which may have the effect of making it very difficult to feel a sense of belonging.

A strong structure or framework not only helps those attending, but also serves as a tool for those who are creating the festival worship. The structure outlined above acts as a kind of mannequin on which the joyful or solemn clothes of the day can be placed. It is then relatively straightforward to look and see if there is too much in places, or whether there are embarrassingly

> A strong structure or framework not only helps those attending, but also serves as a tool for those who are creating the festival worship

9

skimpy bits which will seem awkward in public. The appropriate 'clothes' need to have the capacity to engage people on a number of different levels.

Engaging the senses

The great festivals of Scripture seem to have been events that engaged every human sense. There was music to listen to, the visual spectacle of procession, the smell of burning incense or sacrifice, the taste of the celebration meal and the touch that comes from being with crowds of people. Human beings are multi-sensory, yet many of our church occasions are limited to listening, with some visual elements as well. There are so many imaginative ways of creating worship that uses all the senses, particularly with some of the festivals, where the story we are telling is in itself a multi-sensory experience. Maundy Thursday is one such occasion – there is the possibility of tasting food, touching feet, smelling perfume, experiencing silence, and the visual impact of stripping the altars.

> There are so many imaginative ways of creating worship that uses all the senses, particularly with some of the festivals, where the story we are telling is in itself a multi-sensory experience

Using the senses in worship is sometimes about absence as much as it is about inclusion. The use of stillness and silence in contrast to noise and busyness can be very powerful and dramatic if done well.

Closely related to the possibility of being multi-sensory is also the challenge of using the space more effectively, something for which festivals give particular opportunities. Many of us are blessed with extraordinary buildings, with layer upon layer of history and an abundance of individual stories. Each and every dedication on a tomb or a stained-glass window is a gateway into a person's life, a life that may well have resonances with the challenges we face today. But even without knowing the detail, the colour and texture of walls, windows, ceilings and floors have the potential to be as inspiring as looking forward all the time towards the chancel.

For many younger children, simply being in the transcendent space of a church will be their encounter with God. There will be no need to quantify or explain this – it is an experience of the spirit, not of the mind. Many adults will recollect moments of indescribable beauty experienced sitting in a service they could not understand with their minds, but sensing the flow of sound through words and music, gazing up into a cavernous roof space, spotting tiny angels or glimpses of colour, all of which will speak of God.

Festivals give us the opportunity to utilize outdoor space as well, which might be as simple as using the churchyard or as complex as developing a procession through church and community. The symbolic act of entering the church dramatically after a short period outside can be a powerful reminder of God's invitation. Adults worry a great deal about weather and whether it will stop something happening – younger people tend to be much less concerned, and unless there is an absolute deluge will be unafraid to go out in the rain (and even then teenagers revel in the opportunity to get soaking wet!). It may be that logistics need careful planning, with alternatives for those unable to move well or comfortably, but the experience of being outside is meaningful on many levels. There is the big outdoor space but also the miracle of mini-beasts hiding in the ground and the physical reminder of the community we live in – all these can be part of festival worship.

Mystery and wonder

Movement and multi-sensory activities all contribute towards moments of astonishment in worship – those moments in secular events that we might call the 'wow' factor. In worship this might be expressed in an exultant corporate shout of praise or equally in a profound moment of silence. Mystery and wonder are essential parts of all-age worship, and are at the heart of many of our festivals as we celebrate the unbelievable truth of God's revelation to the world. It is tempting at festivals such as Christmas or Mothering Sunday to fill our worship time with noise and activity, but it is equally important to have moments for reflection which not only allow for different learning styles and

> Mystery and wonder are essential parts of all-age worship, and are at the heart of many of our festivals as we celebrate the unbelievable truth of God's revelation to the world

personality types to engage, but also have the capacity to draw everyone into wonder and contemplation.

There is a myth in churches that says that children cannot concentrate or cannot be still or silent. Children are more than able to concentrate if they are absorbed and engaged, know what is expected and are given a framework in which it happens. Announcing a period of silence (and delivering on the announcement) is more effective for younger children than an open-ended, unexplained vacuum which may or may not last more than a breath. In some of our 'solemn assemblies', notably the great Holy Week liturgies, silence is essential – but this does not mean children have to be excluded. It simply has to be directed well.

The experience of wonder is one of life's universal experiences. A toddler learning to walk will be transfixed by the mystery of a feather on the ground, and a middle-aged woman (me!) is equally awed by the commonplace spectacle of a spider's web stretching over fifteen feet across the garden. Older people will speak of their delight in watching the sun rise and even the coolest teenager will be awed by the extremes of creation.

Universal themes

Stories containing universal themes are another of the key components of successful all-age communications. Pixar films are among the best at doing this, identifying the core concerns of humans and then building them into a story that touches everyone – which is also why these films are eminently re-watchable, like the best childhood books, still appealing to us in adulthood. Questions such as: Am I loved? What happens if I fail? How do I deal with disappointment? What is the purpose of my life? – these are all explored in classic, timeless all-age stories and communications. The great news for those of us trying to create all-age festivals in the local church is that the stories and teachings we are

> The great news for those of us trying to create all-age festivals in the local church is that the stories and teachings we are commemorating are rich in these kinds of universal themes

commemorating are rich in these kinds of universal themes. The task for us is to approach with fresh eyes and identify some of the core issues, whether in the stories of Jesus or the great narratives of the Old Testament.

Tips for preparing and leading

Every word doesn't have to engage every person

The assumption that everyone has to understand a story in the same way or gain a particular experience from worship is an unnecessary pressure that we place on ourselves when we create an all-age service. The space being created with words, music, visuals, activities, is a space of possibilities for encounter, not a learning space for education. In any given act of worship it may be one word or sentence that makes the moment of encounter, or it may be an overall feeling that is created, whereas large tracts of the words and music may be forgotten or ignored. That does not make the worship a failure. A child or adult who goes home after a Palm Sunday procession talking of the way in which everyone held a cross has not missed the point. The point is that there was the potential in the event for encounter – but the mystery is just how the Spirit might work in the lives of the 20 or 200 people present.

Likewise, we don't need to assume that there is one single meaning to any given reading: we may think that the main point of the parable of the Prodigal Son is about the loving father, but for one group I worked with there was a much bigger question about family dynamics and the impact of an absent mother. Family dynamics are universal, while not everyone experiences leaving home with the money!

Prepare and rehearse

All-age festivals in church are about possibilities, and they begin with praying hard and preparing well. Spend time understanding the occasion, researching customs and traditions as well as thinking about all those who might be present. Read the lectionary readings, think about them and look through the worship outline. Take time to think about how suggestions will work in your context with your local congregation. It is good to develop a 'worship planning team' who meet together regularly, and this team should, if possible, include some younger people.

Once a festival outline has been developed, make time to rehearse. It is absolutely normal to have a rehearsal for a wedding service to make sure that the key people are confident about what they need to do on the day, yet we often create complex worship services which involve movement and activity and have no time to practise. Rehearsing drama, readings and prayer as well as movement makes a huge difference to the way in which a service happens, and when it moves with pace and conviction it is much easier for people to be drawn in and engaged.

Music

Most of these outlines do not contain recommended hymns or music. However, music is an important element in our worship, perhaps particularly so during festivals, and the choice of music that is sung by a congregation or by a choir is significant. There may also be opportunities for introducing new music or for listening to contemporary sacred or secular music, especially during times of reflection or intercession. Use the gifts and skills that are present locally across the age ranges, whether playing instruments, singing or composing.

Pre- and post-review

After designing a worship outline, it is good practice to do a mental review of different people in the congregation and ask the question: 'Is there something with the potential to engage Jake, aged 6, here and something for Joan, aged 86? Or are there things that will prevent them engaging –

Note

1 Elizabeth Goudge, *The Little White Horse*, 1946, ch. 9.

too much action, too little movement, etc.?' It doesn't mean that these are the things that will engage them, but that the possibility has been provided. It is also vital to review the worship afterwards, checking where logistics were a problem, where things connected and where they didn't, and reflect on why. This helps to build up a sense of what will work in your context.

Be a leader

During the worship, lead and participate with conviction and commitment, which helps to make sure that the emotional tone of the worship echoes the themes and the words. One of my earliest memories of church (I was not from a churchgoing family, but went to some school events) is pondering the mystery of the words: 'All people that on earth do dwell/sing to the Lord with cheerful voice', which seemed to be sung in the most miserable way imaginable. Even today, it amazes me how easy it is for congregations to give the word 'Alleluia' a meaning akin to 'This is the worst day in my whole life'. This kind of dissonance makes it difficult to experience the full meaning of a festival, particularly one that is meant to be a joyful celebration.

Festivals are an incredible gift to the Church. They can be a tool for mission and evangelism, giving opportunities to engage creatively with the community, but they are also waypoints in our personal discipleship, giving us a chance to encounter the familiar themes and stories in new and challenging ways. Festivals offer opportunities to rekindle faith on a personal level, and yet also to make a visible impact on the community. Festivals really matter to us – so above all, enjoy!

How to use this book

There are fifteen festival outlines in this book, each of them offering something different. They range from the familiar occasions such as Mothering Sunday to the solemn days of Holy Week.[1] The ideas that are offered are jumping-off points, and can be adapted and developed in tune with the local situation. It is important to learn what will work in your environment, both practically and emotionally. There are physical limitations and opportunities that differ, and there are congregations that enjoy some approaches to worship, while other activities can be a stumbling block. Although all of these outlines offer different ideas, in reality it is valuable to build confidence through familiarity. Using the same words is important as it enables people to create a memory bank of sacred texts which they can use with ease, allowing them to experience a sense of belonging.

All the liturgies can be used as eucharistic worship within a common worship framework, and they are based around the relevant lectionary readings. Outlines can be used as a whole, or elements can be used separately, perhaps to introduce new ideas, or to add creativity in different contexts such as school or community worship events. Festivals are also opportunities to take worship into new contexts, perhaps holding services after school or in a village hall, and these outlines can be adapted for these situations.

The outlines that follow are ready to be used. They are not dependent on the presence of children to make them work, but rather designed to help everyone present into worship. You can use them as they are or use them as jumping-off points. If you have never done anything creative in worship before, it's possible to take one section alone and use it. For example, you might decide to introduce a creative way of leading intercessions or a new approach to presenting a reading.

The outlines are built around the structure talked about earlier. These notes should be read in conjunction with the worship outlines.

Title

Each outline has been given a title, which informs the choice of activities and the approach to the content. There is also a short introduction which gives a brief background and ideas about where the outline might be used.

Lectionary

The choice of readings is indicative, taken from the time of year. You will need to use the appropriate readings from the authorized lectionary when the service is the principal service of the day. Check the specific notes for each festival.

Preparation

There may be special areas of the building or outside areas to prepare prior to the worship.

You will need

This section lists the items you will need to source for the worship suggestions. It is a good idea to build up a store of items that are used frequently, and at the end of this section there are some suggestions as to where some items can be sourced.

WE GATHER

Make a note of any suggestions for movement during the opening hymn. There are also suggestions if anything needs to be handed out before the service begins.

Opening hymn

It is good to choose a robust, well-known all-age hymn as the first hymn. If you expect a significant number of those unfamiliar with church, choose those that are lodged within the national psyche (e.g. 'Praise, my soul, the King of heaven') and be mindful of the hymns that parents would have known from school (e.g. 'Lord of the dance'; 'One more step'), as well as those that children are learning today. The music needs to be appropriate for whoever is present – remembering that the wordiness of most hymns precludes non-readers from joining in anyway. A good strong tune where the rhythm can be felt by preschoolers is very helpful.

Opening praise/worship

Where a 'voice' is suggested, this can be anyone of any age and does not need to be an authorized minister.

We say sorry

Within the Church of England, only authorized forms of confession and absolution can be used. All the suggestions in this book conform with this expectation. If a lay person is leading the service they should use the inclusive 'us' form of the absolution.

Making connections

The words set in a panel, to be spoken by/given to whoever is leading the worship service, are suggestions for linking or introducing the worship activities. Please feel free to adapt these words or to be impromptu as appropriate.

The Gloria or hymn

There are many settings of the Gloria to familiar tunes. It is important that the congregation become familiar with the tune and words used or, if there is a choir, this might be an opportunity for the congregation to listen to something fresh. The Gloria is not used during Lent or Advent.

The collect or prayer for the day

In the Church of England, the collect for the day must be used at the principal service of the day and in those seasons where the authorized lectionary must be used. In a 'service of the word' other collects can be written, and *New Patterns for Worship*[2] gives suggestions for writing your own. The prayers in this book are specially written or selected and are not the collect of the day (unless indicated as such).

 **WE LISTEN**

Readings

There are suggestions for presenting readings, and sometimes specific versions or adaptations of a reading are recommended. There are also some original scripts (see the 'Additional resources' that follow some of the outlines). Remember to rehearse any dramatic versions and to practise reading. If you are using more than one reading, don't do elaborate things with each reading. Keep one or two simple, and use just one in a different form.

If the service is a Church of England Eucharist and you are using only one reading, it must be the Gospel.

There are many different versions of the Bible. Some are translations, some are paraphrases and some are story versions. Good translations for regular use are the *Contemporary English Version* or the *New Revised Standard Version*, both of which use inclusive language and are good for reading aloud. (Check whether older editions of translations use inclusive language.) *The Message* is a paraphrase, which sometimes makes a refreshing – and surprising – alternative, particularly for some of the prophets and Psalms. Story versions, for example, *The Lion Storyteller Bible*,[3] *The Book of Books*,[4] *The Big Bible Story Book*[5] and many others, are often helpful. Some story versions of texts are quite lengthy, and will also have a particular interpretive slant, of which you might want to be aware.

The talk

This is a suggestion for an all-age talk based on the readings and the festival. It can be used as a jumping-off point and should be adapted in the light of specific readings and local contexts. (All the talks in this book have been used on different occasions, and frequently adapted!) The text set in a panel provides a suggested outline for a talk.

Hymn

Many services will include a hymn or song somewhere in this part of the service. In a formal service it may be known as a 'gradual hymn' (but many church attenders have no idea what this word means, and it should be avoided for all-age services). This hymn should be a shorter, more direct hymn that reflects the readings.

 WE RESPOND

We believe

Each outline offers a suggestion for a creed or affirmation of faith. This has to be included in a Church of England principal service on a Sunday but is not essential in a service of the word. The form used must be authorized, and the majority of the outlines in this book use the same form each time. This is to help build a sense of familiarity and belonging, but it is appropriate to use an alternative, particularly during special seasons of the church year. There is also a 'making connections' suggestion, words in a panel, spoken by the minister/leader, which can be adapted as an introduction.

Prayer ideas

Most outlines contain two creative ways of praying, one of which will be static, word-based and simpler, while the other may involve movement. Sometimes these will require preparation beforehand, for example, creating prayer stations and providing objects or materials for people to use.

The prayers can be led by one or more voices, and handing the ideas to a family or a prayer group so they can prepare can be a good way of developing skills and involving more people in leading intercessions. Sometimes the prayers involve movement, and it is a good idea to have one person directing and modelling the movements while someone else says the words. If the prayer activity involves people moving around the worship space, it is helpful to play suitable music. This could be played by a worship group or organist, but it is also an opportunity to use recorded music. This needs to be selected with care. If there are lyrics, then they will need to complement the prayer focus rather than distract, and the mood of the piece needs to complement the mood of the prayers. If people are being encouraged to think about sadness, then blasting out 'Oh Lord, I wanna sing your praises' is jarring but, equally, playing a haunting melody when the focus is on praying for joy in various situations may be distracting.

Although this book contains different ideas and approaches for each month, in reality you will find that certain approaches to prayer work well in specific contexts. Some congregations find prayer stations impossible, others really enjoy them. Likewise some worship leaders find they have a gift for encouraging movement in prayer, whereas others find the use of objects to be helpful. Doing something new and exciting every time is not the key to good inclusive worship, so don't feel obliged to keep introducing different ideas. Find a few ways that work and stick with them for a while, then maybe introduce something different for a special occasion.

If the service is a service of the word, it is appropriate to end the prayers with the Lord's Prayer.

The peace

Although not essential in a non-eucharistic service, exchanging the peace is a lovely moment of inclusion and acknowledging that we are gathered as the whole people of God. Various words can be used to introduce the peace, but the formal words 'the peace of the Lord be always with you' must be included and said by an authorized minister.

We celebrate

There are no specific suggestions offered in the outlines for the Eucharist, although it is recommended that in the Church of England, Prayer D from *Common Worship*[6] be used (or one of the new eucharistic prayers for use with children present, once authorized) and that thought be given to the mechanics of distribution as well as the prayers.

It is also good to involve children and adults together in bringing the gifts to the altar and also in preparing the table. A hymn is usually sung while this is happening, and it needs to be of sufficient length to allow for all the activity to take place.

➡️ WE GO OUT

This section has ideas for sending out into the world, and alternative blessing prayers. Sometimes the dismissal involves handing things out to people, so it is important to have prepared this. As with earlier sections, where it says 'voice', any person can take part. Blessings should be said by an authorized minister, and those offered in this book are suggestions. There are many options available.

Final hymn

As with the opening hymn, it is good to choose something that has a strong, familiar tune. The first impression and the last impression are very important, so it's good if people leave feeling positive. The music will also need to fit with the style of the service. 'You shall go out with joy' may be great with an informal ending, but less suitable for a formal exit where a more traditional style will be more appropriate.

Whether you decide to use these ideas and themes, or to create your own, the intention is to create the kind of worship where each person leaves feeling excited or moved by all that has happened, and each member of the church family and the domestic family feels positive about their experience. And at the next 'all-age service' the people will be coming down the path full of anticipation, glad to be coming to church, knowing that there will be something welcoming and relevant happening!

Where to source things

- *Pebbles and decorative items* Stores such as IKEA, Dunelm Mill, Wilkinson and local discount stores are good for these kinds of items.
- *Silk flowers* As above, also markets.
- *Paper hearts and other craft materials* Pre-cut are available from craft retailers such as Hobbycraft, and also through Baker Ross and similar online companies.
- A *map of the world* Good large plastic maps are available from toy shops. There are specialist map stores online.
- *Confetti* Different types of shiny confetti are available in most card shops, specialist party stores and in local markets.
- *Fabric* Try local Asian fabric stores, markets or Dunelm Mill. Sheer fabrics are good, as are lining materials – buy lengths of around five metres as this drapes well over tables, pulpits, etc. and is a good length for moving around the church.
- *Ribbons* Markets, haberdashers, etc.
- *Images* can generally be sourced through an 'image' search on the Internet.
- Many areas of the country have local authority *'scrap-stores'* – places that sell recyclable materials from local manufacturers to charities, schools and community groups. You can usually fill a shopping trolley for around £15. These are not so good for specific items and quantities at short notice, but worth browsing to build up a stock of potentially useful items.
- *DIY stores* are also full of useful things, as are second-hand stores and gift shops.

Notes

1 There are no services for Epiphany or Advent in this book – the services for January and December in the companion volume, *Worship Together*, may be used for these occasions.
2 *New Patterns for Worship*, London: Church House Publishing, 2008.
3 Bob Hartman and Krisztina Kallai Nagy, *The Lion Storyteller Bible*, Oxford: Lion Hudson, 2008.
4 Trevor Dennis, *The Book of Books*, Oxford: Lion Hudson, 2009.
5 Maggie Barfield, *The Big Bible Story Book: 188 Bible Stories to Enjoy Together*, Bletchley: Scripture Union, 2007.
6 'This is our story, this is our song', *Common Worship: Services and Prayers for the Church of England*, London: Church House Publishing, 2000, p. 194.

Part 2

The service outlines

Looking back, moving on

Candlemas is a festival full of Christian symbolism, folk tradition and church history, which means there is a wealth of images and themes to explore. It marks a turning point in three ways – within the Church it is the moment we take a last look at Christmas and the infant Jesus before turning towards the cross; in the northern hemisphere it marks the turning from winter towards spring; and it also marks the shift from darkness to light. It is called Candlemas because long ago churches would bless all the candles which would be used throughout the church year, a tradition adapted in this outline. There are several folk sayings and traditions linked to Candlemas, some of which pick up the themes of change and transition.

Although the date for this festival is 2 February, it can be moved to the nearest Sunday, but it might also be a good occasion to try some all-age worship mid-week, perhaps after school, using the school facilities or church. It is amazing that in a technological age there is still something both exciting and entrancing for children about candles – and a risk element connected with lighting them! However, it is a manageable risk, and with careful planning, lighting candles can be included in an event involving children.

Key lectionary readings

NB: Please see note on lectionary readings in 'How to use this book' (p. 13).

If Candlemas is celebrated as a principal service in Epiphany, then the lectionary readings must be used.

Malachi 3.1–5 'Judging with purity'
Hebrews 2.14–18 'The one who saves'
Luke 2.22–40 'A light to reveal'

Preparation

You will need

- A large map of the world or globe; a large candle
- A bag containing a small Christmas tree, a small nativity scene, a picture of a starry night (downloaded from the Internet)
- A second bag containing an Easter egg, a small cross, a picture of a dawn (downloaded from the Internet)
- Two other large candles
- Optional: small candles, e.g. tealights, two per person

 ## WE GATHER

Opening hymn

Place a large map of the world (or a large globe) at the front of the worship space.

During the first hymn, make a procession through the church carrying the first of the large candles.

Turn and face the people gathered.

Informal welcome

Formal introduction

Minister	The Lord be with you.
All	**And also with you.**
Voice	Jesus is the light of the world. Come, let us worship.
All	**Come, let us worship.**

Voice Jesus is light in our lives. Come, let us worship.

All **Come, let us worship.**

Place the first large candle in the middle of the world map or in front of the globe.

We say sorry

Making connections

Minister Light shows up things that have been forgotten or lost or hidden. As we come into Jesus' presence, his light reminds us of all the good things we have forgotten to do and all the things that we have hidden away. But if we say sorry, then we can walk in the light.

So let's take a few moments now to say sorry to God.

(*Turn lights down low and invite those who wish to find a quiet space, which might mean putting head in hands or curling up in a ball.*)

Minister As we sit in the darkness we remember.

Voice For all the times we have ignored people in need, Lord, have mercy.

All **Lord, have mercy.**

Voice For all the times we have deliberately made wrong choices,
Christ, have mercy.

All **Christ, have mercy.**

Voice For all the times we have forgotten your love, Lord, have mercy.

All **Lord, have mercy.**

(*Allow a few moments of silence before turning lights up and saying the absolution.*)

Minister May the God of love
bring *us* back to himself,
forgive *us our* sins,
and assure *us* of his eternal love
in Jesus Christ our Lord.

All **Amen.**[1]

Hymn/Gloria

Collect for Candlemas

NB: Please see the note on the collect or prayer for the day in 'How to use this book' (p. 14).

OR

Minister Lord Jesus Christ,
Light of the world,

shine among us and within us;
turn us from darkness
and bring us to your eternal light,
through Jesus Christ our Lord.

All **Amen.**

 **WE LISTEN**

Reading(s)

First reading and second reading: read in a contemporary version.

Gospel: there are many story versions of this passage or see 'Additional resource: Candlemas' at the end of this outline (p. 23) for a mini-drama.

Talk

Invite up to six volunteers to stand in equal numbers on either side of you.

Open the first bag and hand the small Christmas tree to one of the people on the left. Talk about why it's strange to have a Christmas tree – it all seems a long time ago, everything has been put away.

Take out the nativity scene and hand it to one of the people on the left – is it just as strange to look at Jesus as a baby? Explain that today we are looking at Jesus the baby for one last time this winter.

Take out the picture of a starry night and hand it to one of the people on the left. Explain that, as Mary and Joseph bring Jesus into the temple, we are reminded of all that happened up to that point – a night sky full of angels, stars that led strangers to worship, mystery in the night-time. Say something similar to:

When Simeon sees the baby, his mind also fills with ideas of light.

Hand the second large candle to one of the people on the left. Say that Simeon saw that Jesus would be a light for the whole world.

But there is a journey to make from the starry night to the light of the world.

Open the second bag and hand the Easter egg to one of the people on the right. Talk about why it might be strange to have an Easter egg on a cold February day (although they will have been on sale since 26 December!). It seems too soon.

Take out the cross and hand it to one of the people on the right: ask if it seems strange to begin thinking about the cross.

Take out the picture of the dawn and hand it to one of the people on the right.

> We are looking forward to the new light that will dawn on the world, the morning when Jesus is risen from the dead. We are looking forward to angels declaring good news, astonished disciples and mystery in the morning.

> When Simeon sees the baby, his mind is filled with ideas of light.

Hand the third large candle to a volunteer on the right. Talk about the fact that Simeon speaks about Jesus as a light for the whole world.

> But there is a journey to make between these two points. And Simeon saw something of the journey too. He knew that light shows up things that people would rather keep hidden. He knew, just like the old prophets knew, that God's special person would make people feel uncomfortable – exposed. People don't like things hidden being brought into the light. Simeon spoke about these things.

Draw attention to the words Simeon spoke to Mary: 'The inner thoughts of many will be revealed – and a sword shall pierce your heart also.'

Place the cross in the middle, between the Christmas items and the Easter items.

> Today we are looking back to the manger – remembering that Jesus is the light of the world.

> But we are also looking forward to the cross – and beyond, remembering that Jesus is the light for the world that will never fade away.

Place one of the large candles in front of the cross.

> It's just that to get there we will have to go the way of the cross.

> Candlemas is a day of remembering and day of hope – a day to remember that winter will pass and spring will come, and that Jesus' light will always be with us.

 ## WE RESPOND

Creed or statement of faith

Making connections

Minister (or child)   Let's remind ourselves that we are all people of light, believing in the same things, sharing the same love:

All   **We believe in God the Father,**
from whom every family
in heaven and on earth is named.

We believe in God the Son,
who lives in our hearts through faith,
and fills us with his love.

We believe in God the Holy Spirit,
who strengthens us
with power from on high.

We believe in one God;
Father, Son and Holy Spirit.
Amen.[2]

Prayers

If space allows, encourage people to come forward to light a small candle as a sign of their prayers or tealight, or alternatively arrange for individuals to carry candles forward in response to each section of the prayers. These prayers are a series of biddings and responses and can be adapted.

In the pause after each section, invite people to come forward to light candles or ask someone you chose earlier to light one of the large candles.

You could also accompany the response with simple actions. For example:

'We pray' – hold hands out with palms upwards

'to you' – point index finger upwards.

Voice   That our church might be a place full of light, we pray to you, God of light.

All   **We pray to you.**

Voice   That our homes may be places full of love, we pray to you, God of light.

All   **We pray to you.**

Voice   That our schools, places of work and places of fun may be places of joy, we pray to you, God of light.

All   **We pray to you.**

Voice	That those who are in pain or sadness may discover hope, we pray to you, God of light.
All	**We pray to you.**
Voice	That our community and our nation may be led in righteousness, we pray to you, God of light.
All	**We pray to you.**
Voice	That men, women and children in our world may live their lives in peace, we pray to you, God of light.
All	**We pray to you.**
Voice	That each of us might walk in your light every day, we pray to you, O Lord.
All	**We pray to you.**

If the service is a service of the word, it may be appropriate to end the prayers with the Lord's Prayer, before sharing the peace together.

If the service is a Eucharist, continue with the peace followed by the offertory and the eucharistic prayer. Involve different generations as appropriate.

The peace

Introduce the peace, using these or similar words:

Minister	God makes peace within us – let us claim it. God makes peace between us – let us share it. The peace of the Lord be with you
All	**and also with you.**[3]

Notes

1 *New Patterns for Worship*, London: Church House Publishing, 2008, p. 95, B73.
2 *New Patterns for Worship*, p. 166, E12.
3 The St Hilda Community, *New Women Included: A Book of Services and Prayers*, London: SPCK, 1996, p. 55.

 **WE GO OUT**

Notices may be included at this point as part of moving the focus to our Christian lives.

Blessing of candles

Two or more people bring forward two baskets, one containing all the candles that will be used in the church during the year; the other containing enough small candles or tealights for each person in the congregation.

Minister	Lord God, who came as light to the whole world, bless these candles that they might shine with your light, in our church, in our homes, in our worship, leading us towards you, and reminding everyone of your love. Amen.

As people leave, hand out a candle to each person.

Blessing

Minister	May the light of God's love shine in your home and shine in your heart, and the blessing of God, Father, Son and Holy Spirit, be with you, this day and always.
All	**Amen.**

Seeing light

(This may be used instead of the Gospel reading.)

You will need someone with a big torch standing in the pulpit. This person might also be the reader, or you could use a different voice.

Mary and Joseph, holding the baby, are in the shadows at the back of the space.

Simeon and Anna are hidden at the front.

Reader Tick-tock. Tick-tock. Tick-tock. The days are passing since the baby was born.

And now it's time. Look! (*Shine the torch on to Mary and Joseph.*) Look – they are making their way to the temple, walking carefully, slowly, into God's house.

(*Mary and Joseph move down the aisle, with the torch beam following their movements.*)

(*The torch flashes to where Simeon is hiding, and he begins to move forward.*)

Reader Look! Look! Someone is coming forward, slowly, slowly.

(*The two groups meet.*)

Reader Aah! Simeon is looking at the baby. (*Shine the light directly on Jesus.*)

Reader What is it that he sees?

Simeon I can now go in peace! I have seen what I have waited to see. My own eyes can see God's salvation, a light for the whole world, a light for God's people, Israel.

(*Mary and Joseph look at each other amazed. Flash the light straight into Simeon's face.*)

Simeon Aagh! (*Puts hand on Mary.*) This baby will disturb many people. His light will be like a sign. And a sword will pierce your heart as well. You will be made very sad.

(*Pick out Anna with torchlight.*)

Reader Then a prophet called Anna, who had been in the temple day after day worshipping and praying, praying and waiting, came forward praising God and echoing all that Simeon had seen.

(*All stand still at front in a tableau as the light plays on them, and then rests on Jesus, and, if there is a cross somewhere in the space, finally resting on the cross.*)

Mothering Sunday

Who's the mummy?

The celebration of Mothering Sunday has changed greatly over the past decades. In some parishes it remains one of the days when a high number of occasional churchgoers can be expected, but in others it has been superseded by the commercial 'Mother's Day'. For many families, the main focus of the day is treating Mum – so getting up early to go to church is not on the agenda! For those who do come to church there might be mixed emotions – many older people will no longer have a mother. Others may be separated, even estranged, from children, while others struggle with childlessness. Alongside all this are the cultural stereotypes about mothers which may not sit easily with a church which knows God as both father and mother, and which embraces the joys and pains of life.

This service could be used at a time other than Sunday morning, and includes traditional elements as well as making space to acknowledge the mixed feelings that people bring.

Key lectionary readings

NB: Please see note on lectionary readings in 'How to use this book' (p. 13).

Lent is a season that requires the set lectionary readings for the day in a Church of England principal service.

Exodus 2.1–10 'Mothers and others'
Psalm 34.11–20 'God the rescuer'
Colossians 3.12–17 'How to live'
John 19.25–27 'Mothering others'

Preparation

You will need

- A CD of suitable music, e.g. 'All for the love' by Beth Neilson-Chapman
- Enough small flat stones for everyone
- A large pink designer-style handbag containing pink chocolate hearts, a pink fluffy toy, pink bath salts, a romantic novel or DVD, a pink coffee mug, some fancy make-up in a pink case
- A scruffy carrier bag containing an old purse with a few coins, a plate, a tea towel or floor cloth, scruffy bit of children's clothing, sticking plaster, tissues, small blanket
- Five small flower vases each containing a single rose or some simple garden flowers
- According to local custom, flowers to give away

WE GATHER

Opening hymn

Informal welcome

Formal introduction

Minister	The Lord be with you
All	**and also with you.**
Voice	When God's people pray for help
All	**help us today.**
Voice	When God's people pray for help, God listens
All	**hear us today.**
Voice	When God's people pray for help, God listens and rescues them

All	**rescue us today.**
Voice	When God's people pray for help, God listens and rescues them from their troubles.
All	**Amen!**

We say sorry

Making connections

Minister	In all our services we take time to think about things that have gone wrong, even on a happy day like this. Mothering Sunday is not happy for everyone: some people here might not have a mother any more, some might be unable to be mothers, some may have lost a child through death, or lost contact with a child for any number of reasons. Others may have had an unhappy childhood and have painful memories. So as part of saying sorry we are going to think of these situations. After the words have been said, we will listen to some music, and during the song please come up, pick up a stone and place it in front of the altar, where we will build a kind of cairn, which is a special pile of stones to help remember things.

The following could be read by several voices:

Voice	We pray for those who might be sad because they have no children. Lord, have mercy.
All	**Christ, have mercy.**
Voice	We are sad for those who have no mother. Lord, have mercy.
All	**Christ, have mercy.**
Voice	We are sad because we have been hurt by others. Lord, have mercy.
All	**Christ, have mercy.**
Voice	We are sad for all the hurts in God's world. Lord, have mercy.
All	**Christ, have mercy.** *(After these words play music, e.g. 'All for the love' by Beth Neilson-Chapman, and invite people to come forward and build the cairn. When everyone has returned to their seats:)*
Voice	We are sorry because we have hurt other people. Lord, have mercy.
All	**Lord, have mercy.**
Voice	We are sorry that we have ignored the needs of the world. Christ, have mercy.
All	**Christ, have mercy.**

Voice	We are sorry that we have forgotten God's great love for us. Lord, have mercy.
All	**Lord, have mercy.**
Minister	May the God of love and power forgive *us* and free *us* from *our* sins, heal and strengthen *us* by his Spirit, and raise *us* to new life in Christ our Lord.
All	**Amen.**[1]

Hymn

NB: No Gloria in Lent.

Collect for Mothering Sunday

NB: Please see note on the collect or prayer for the day in 'How to use this book' (p. 14).

Voice	Loving God, You sent your Son to be part of a human family. Strengthen us as we share family life together, in our homes and in our church, through Jesus Christ our Lord.
All	**Amen.**

 **WE LISTEN**

Reading(s)

Suggestion: if using only two readings, choose Exodus and John.

The Exodus reading could be read from a story Bible or see 'Additional resource: Mothering Sunday' at the end of this outline (p. 28) for an alternative version.

Talk

Begin by saying that you have been doing some research in the shops to see what kind of person is a mummy. In the pink handbag, there is a collection of things you have found that help you describe the yummy mummy. Remove the items slowly, talking about them as you go:

Yummy mummies seem to lounge around in a nice pink bath, eating nice pink chocolates, reading romances, drinking coffee, then putting on their lovely make-up before going out in their designer clothes with their pink bags. Oh, and they are always soft and cuddly, just like the fluffy toy!

When that picture has been painted, explain that it just seems a bit far removed from real life. Ask mums if that's really what life is like!

Then produce the scruffy carrier bag – the bag belonging to a real mummy. Remove the items, talking about them as you go.

> She doesn't have much time to dress up and think of herself. She is always making sure that there is enough money to go round, cooking the meals, doing the shopping, cleaning the house, washing the clothes. She is there when there is an injury, wipes away the tears . . . oh, and is there to give a cuddle when needed (*show the blanket*).
>
> Being a real mummy is not always easy, it's not always pretty. Sometimes there are other people who are not mothers but show us this kind of love. There are dads and aunties and friends and grandparents. I'm sure you can think of others. In the story of Moses, there were midwives who helped make sure the babies lived, there was his sister who spoke up for him and there was a princess who adopted him, as well as his mother who nursed him and all the others in his family who loved him.
>
> This kind of love is an echo for us of God's love for us – God takes care of us, meets our needs, helps us when we make a mess, holds us when we hurt, and loves us come what may. God is like a mother!
>
> Today is a day to say thank you for all the different ways we have known love – through our mothers and through others as well. It is a time to remember God's love for us all and to think about how we might show that love to other people.

 **WE RESPOND**

Creed or statement of faith

Making connections

Minister	Today we think especially about being part of a family, and particularly of how God is a mother to us. Let's share together in these words:
All	**We believe in God the Father** [and mother], **from whom every family in heaven and on earth is named.**

We believe in God the Son, who lives in our hearts through faith, and fills us with his love.

We believe in God the Holy Spirit, who strengthens us with power from on high.

We believe in one God; Father, Son and Holy Spirit. Amen.[2]

Prayers

You will need the five small vases each containing either a single rose or some simple garden flowers appropriate for Mothering Sunday. Each vase is to be carried by someone of a different generation (if possible).

Oldest person e.g. a great-grandmother or great-grandfather (If this person cannot walk forward easily, a younger person could take the vase and bring it forward.)   Loving God, we give

> thanks for the great love you have for each of us. We pray that you will help each of us pass that love on to the next generation.
> Lord, hear our prayer

All	**please.**

An adult mother/father   Loving God, we give thanks for all mothers and for everything they do, or once did for us, and for all that they mean to us today. We also pray for those who are without family today, for whatever reason, and ask that you would help them to know your love is always close.
Lord, hear our prayer

All	**please.**

A young family   Loving God, we thank you for family life. We pray for those who are waiting for a new baby, and beginning family life. We pray especially for those who are trying to make home and family in difficult circumstances, especially in places of war and struggle.
Lord, hear our prayer

All	**please.**

A teenager   Loving God, we thank you for the family of the church. We pray for those who welcome others, who encourage and bless. Inspire us in our worship, and give us a new vision to show your love to those around us.
Lord, hear our prayer

All	**please.**

A child   Loving God, thank you for everybody who looks after other people. Help us to know that you are

always with each one of us.
Lord, hear our prayer

All   **please.**

If the service is a service of the word, it may be appropriate to end the prayers with the Lord's Prayer, before sharing the peace together.

If the service is a Eucharist, continue with the peace followed by the offertory and the eucharistic prayer. Involve different generations as appropriate.

The peace

Introduce the peace, using these or similar words:

Minister   God makes peace within us – let us claim it.
             God makes peace between us – let us share it.
             The peace of the Lord be with you

All   **and also with you.**[3]

 **WE GO OUT**

Notices may be included at this point as part of moving the focus to our Christian lives.

Notes

1 *New Patterns for Worship*, London: Church House Publishing, 2008, p. 97, B80.
2 *New Patterns for Worship,* p. 166, E12.
3 The St Hilda Community, *New Women Included: A Book of Services and Prayers*, London: SPCK, 1996, p. 55.

Blessing of flowers

Bring forward baskets with flowers and pray a blessing:

Minister   Loving God, who is both our father and our mother,
             we thank you for all the love we have known in our homes, among our friends, with God's people.
             Bless these flowers and, as we share them, may they remind us to be people of thanks, people of love, and people of joy in Jesus' name.
             Amen.

Blessing

Minister   May God who made the whole earth, bless us (*make huge circle with arms*).
             May God who draws us all together, bless us (*make hug across body*).
             May God who loves each one of us, bless us (*place hand on heart*).
             And the blessing of God,
             Father, Son and Holy Spirit,
             be with you, and all whom you love,
             this day and always.

All   **Amen.**

Exodus 2.1–10 alternative version

You will need two people as narrators, and four or five others to speak; and a baby doll in a basket.

If possible, characters could dress up, or simply carry cards with their names on.

Voice 1 It takes a lot of people to make sure a baby lives and grows.

Voice 2 It takes a lot of people to love.

(*Place the doll in the basket at the front, with the four speakers indicated below standing round.*)

Midwives There are brave midwives, who stand up to power, who speak boldly to the Pharaohs in our world, who have courage and make sure the babies LIVE! That's what we did for the Hebrew families – and God blessed us.

Mother There are mothers, who watch and wait and worry, and when the time is right step out and take a risk, making the baby as safe as possible, carefully, tearfully, placing him in the river. That's what I did for my special baby – and God saw me.

Pharaoh's daughter There are princesses like me, and paupers too, women without children, who care, sometimes fostering, sometimes teaching, but always loving. That's what I did for that precious baby boy – and God was with me.

Miriam There are sisters and aunts and friends and ministers, women who speak out when others are silent, who demand things for children when others turn away, who are passionate and bold and strong. That's what I did for my little baby brother – and God heard me.

Voice 1 It took a lot of people to make sure that baby Moses lived and grew.

Voice 2 It took a lot of people to show a mother's love.

Festivals Together (London: SPCK). Copyright © Sandra Millar 2012

Palm Sunday

Parade with passion

The Palm Sunday procession marks the beginning of the greatest week in the church calendar, the week when we engage again with the story of Jesus' journey to the cross and beyond. The story is so powerful and contains so many core images and motifs that shape our beliefs, and it presents an opportunity for all ages to encounter the mystery of faith.

Palm Sunday might seem the easiest Sunday on which to create all-age worship – simply bring in a donkey and the job's done! But the Palm Sunday readings encourage us not only to engage with Jesus acclaimed as king, but also to take a panoramic view of the whole passion story before engaging with it in detail during the week ahead. It's as if we are taken to a high point on a mountain where we look down at everything that lies ahead.

This worship service tries to capture that sense. It is designed as a procession – with or without a donkey – but if it is not possible for physical movement from place to place, it could also be created using the internal worship space. The talk is split into short comments at each location, based on the 'episode' drama at the end. It is possible to combine the readings if you have fewer stops, and an alternative structure is provided.

Key lectionary readings

NB: Please see note on lectionary readings in 'How to use this book' (p. 13).

Lent is a season that requires the set lectionary readings for the day in a Church of England principal service.

Psalm 118.19–24 'Open the gates'
Matthew 21.1–11 'This is your King'
OR
Isaiah 50.4–9a 'The suffering servant'
Psalm 31.9–16 'The pain of life'
Philippians 2.5–11 'Be like this'
Matthew 26.14—27.66 'The end game'

Preparation

You will need

- Large branches and enough palm crosses for one each
- Lots of metal paper clips, not plastic coloured ones

 ## WE GATHER

This should be outside, at the starting point of the procession. If you are not processing, gather everyone outside the door and then process into the church.

Opening hymn

Informal welcome

Formal introduction

Minister   The Lord be with you
All   **and also with you.**

If you have a choir, you could rehearse this to look like a 'flash choir'. One by one people start singing in unexpected places, until a whole group has joined in, for example: 'We will enter his gates with thanksgiving in our hearts'.

Voice	We will enter his gates with thanksgiving in our hearts
All	**We will enter**
Voice	With thanksgiving
All	**With thanksgiving**
Voice	For the Lord is a mighty God
All	**A mighty God**
Voice	Hosanna!
All	**Hosanna!**

Sing chorus 'We will enter' or similar.

Blessing of palms

Voice	Hosanna! Sound the trumpet, clap your hands, wave the palms high!
Minister	We bless these palms and remember Jesus our Messiah, humble and riding on a donkey. May they be a sign to us of the Servant King. As we carry them, may they remind us to walk the way that leads to life. Hosanna!
All	**Amen! Hosanna!**
Voice	Let's go, shouting praises to Jesus our Messiah!

Stop 1

We say sorry

Read Isaiah 50.4–9a.

> ### *Making connections*

Minister	It was a great day to be shouting praises to Jesus. For a moment everyone thought he was the King they were expecting . . . but then the crowds drifted away and the disappointment set in. People began to moan and grumble because nothing seemed to change. They hadn't understood just what was going to happen. They hadn't understood just how big the plan was – Jesus is the Saviour of the world.

We forget too. We shout and sing, but too often our praises turn to grumbles. We forget that Jesus is the Saviour of the world. Let's stand in the silence, and look at the palm cross for a moment. |
| *Voice 1* | Lord God, it's easy to wave the cross in praise but hard to give you thanks every day. Forgive us for our selfishness and greed. Lord, have mercy. |

All	**Lord, have mercy.**
Voice 2	Lord God, it's easy to hold a palm cross, but we forget that Jesus is the Saviour of the world. Forgive us for our laziness and neglect. Christ, have mercy.
All	**Christ, have mercy.**
Voice 3	It's easy to have a cross for a day, but we forget that we are called to take up our cross every day. Forgive us for going our own way. Lord, have mercy.
All	**Lord, have mercy.**
Minister	May almighty God, who sent his Son into the world to save sinners, bring *us* his pardon and peace, now and for ever.
All	**Amen.**[1]

Hymn

To be sung while processing to the next stop.

WE LISTEN AND RESPOND

Stop 2

Reading(s)

For text, see 'Additional resource: Palm Sunday 1' at the end of this outline (p. 33).

Episode 1: The meal

Ask people to think for a moment about what makes an occasion memorable. It might be what we eat, or do, but often it is when the unexpected happens – when it pours with rain at a picnic or when someone makes a surprising speech. Jesus was celebrating the Passover, a meal that God's people had celebrated for centuries, but he did surprising things. He washed feet and told them that bread and wine would always remind them of his death.

Invite people to gather in groups of eight to ten. Pass the sign of the cross around the group EITHER by making the sign of the cross on the palms of one another's hands OR by passing round one of the palm crosses, each time saying: 'Remember all that Jesus did.'

Voice	Lord God, thank you for the stories you told, the things you did, the words you said. Help us,

your Church, to remember well all that your life and death mean, and to live our lives serving other people.

All   **Amen.**

(*It may be appropriate to move between each of these sections.*)

Stop 3

Reading

For text, see 'Additional resource: Palm Sunday 1' at the end of this outline (p. 33).

Episode 2: The arrest

Talk about how it was all going wrong in contrast to the hopes that people had when Jesus entered Jerusalem. When things start going wrong, people can behave badly. Ask for examples. Jesus' friends were frightened. They let him down, they fell asleep, they ran away. Judas betrayed him.

Invite people to gather into small huddles of three or four as we pray for friends and families.

Voice   Lord God, thank you that you call us to live in families and communities. We pray for our friends and those we love, especially those who may be struggling with difficulties. Help us to be strong and faithful in helping others. Amen.

Stop 4

Reading

For text, see 'Additional resource: Palm Sunday 1' at the end of this outline (p. 34).

Episode 3: The trials

Minister   It's not easy to be treated unfairly. How many people have ever been blamed wrongly – at school or at home? It's so unfair. Sometimes we are even punished for something we know we didn't do. Jesus' trial was unfair. Things were going very wrong. He was alone.

(*Hand out the piles of metal paper clips and invite people in pairs to make a long chain of clips to represent those things that unfairly affect people as we pray for the world. Pray for people who are suffering because of injustice and violence and ask God to be with them.*)

Voice   Lord God, we pray for our world, and especially those places where there is injustice. Give courage to those who are struggling to work for peace and speak out for truth. Strengthen all of us as we work to see your kingdom come.
Amen.

Stop 5

Reading

For text, see 'Additional resource: Palm Sunday 1' at the end of this outline (p. 34).

Episode 4: The death

Minister   It seems a long way now from the joyful shouts of Hosanna. But this is the story of Holy Week, the story we have to follow now before we get to the joy of Easter Day. Let's sit quietly for a moment and ask God to help each of us to discover more this week of his great love.

(*Invite people to place a hand on their heart and a hand over their eyes and simply pray silently.*)

Voice   Lord God, hear our prayers and help us to follow you.
Amen.

If this is a Eucharist, share the peace before beginning to move into the church; if a service of the word, then share the peace when all are in the church.

The peace

Introduce the peace, using these or similar words:

Minister   Jesus says: 'Peace I leave with you; my peace I give to you.
Do not let your hearts be troubled, neither let them be afraid.'
The peace of the Lord be with you

All   **and also with you.**[2]

If the service is a Eucharist, move procession into the church, and sing a hymn while the offertory is taken before continuing with the eucharistic prayer.

We celebrate

 WE GO OUT

Notices may be included at this point as part of moving the focus to our Christian lives.

Blessing

Minister	May the love of God go with you,
	grace and peace surround you,
	may the hope of the cross inspire you,
	joy and gladness fill your lives.
	And the blessing of God,
	Father, Son and Holy Spirit,
	be with you this day and always.
All	**Amen.**

Voice   Christ was humble. He obeyed God and even died on a cross. Then God gave Christ the highest place and honoured his name above all others (*Philippians 2.8–9*). Think the same way that Jesus thought.

All   **Let's make our hearts ready** (*place clenched fist over heart and tap twice*)

All   **to follow Jesus our King** (*use both arms to make cross sign*).

Notes

1 *New Patterns for Worship*, London: Church House Publishing, 2008, p. 95, B72, from the prayer beginning 'The Lord enrich you with his grace', in *In Penitence and Faith: Texts for Use with Alternative Services*, compiled by David Silk. Reproduced by permission of Continuum International Publishing Group.

2 *New Patterns for Worship*, p. 273, H9.

The Passion in four episodes

These readings are designed to be used at each of the 'stops' in a procession. If appropriate, they could be read by people in costume. You will need four readers.

Episode 1: The meal

It was the beginning of Passover and Jesus told us to get the meal ready. We all met in a room upstairs. At first it was like any other Passover meal. But then the first unusual thing happened.

We were all waiting for the slave to wash our feet, when Jesus took the towel from her, gently pushed her to one side, knelt down and began to wash our feet. We were so shocked that we couldn't find words to say. But when he got to Peter, Peter spoke: 'You can't do this for me, Jesus. You just can't.'

But Jesus insisted. He insisted that what he was doing was special. So he washed Peter's feet, and then finished washing all our feet. He sat back and looked at us, and said: 'If I, your teacher and your Lord, wash your feet, then you must do this for other people.'

Next Jesus suggested that one of us would betray him . . . and Judas slipped out of the room.

But that wasn't the only odd thing to happen.

Jesus took the bread, broke it and thanked God. He gave it to us and said: 'This is my body . . .' Then he took the cup with wine in it, thanked God, and asked us to drink it. He said: 'This is my blood, which is given for many people. In the future, every time you do this, remember me.'

The mood had definitely shifted. Jesus began to talk about dying and as usual Peter jumped in. He announced that he would stick with Jesus, whatever happened . . . but Jesus said that before the night was over, Peter would let him down, not once, but three times.

It was a very strange meal.

Episode 2: The arrest

The disciples left the room and went to Gethsemane to pray. Most of them stayed in the background, but Peter, James and John were close to Jesus. As Jesus kept on praying, they kept on falling asleep, until Jesus was left alone, praying intensely, asking God to help him to do what God wanted. Eventually, Jesus came and woke them up: 'It's time,' he said.

Even as he was speaking Judas came up. There was a mob of armed men with him. He walked over and kissed Jesus . . . and the armed men came and arrested Jesus. One of Jesus' followers was so angry, he cut off the ear of one of the men. But Jesus said: 'This is the way things have to be.' And they led him away to be questioned.

Some disciples followed. But some ran away. Peter went right into the courtyard to find out what was happening. He was trying not to be noticed, but a serving woman saw him. 'Hey, you!' she cried. 'Aren't you with the man from Nazareth?'

'No!' growled Peter.

Festivals Together (London: SPCK). Copyright © Sandra Millar 2012

She saw him again a bit later and said: 'You are one of them!'

'No, I am not,' said Peter, very firmly. He slipped further into the shadows.

But a little while later some people noticed him and said: 'You are definitely one of them! We can tell by your accent!'

'I am not!' yelled Peter. 'I have told you once, and I'm telling you now: I don't know him!'

Then a cock crowed three times and Peter remembered all that Jesus had said.

He simply began to cry.

Episode 3: The trials

The night became very confusing. People were rushing about all over the city, waking up the priest, waking up Herod, waking up the Roman ruler. Jesus was pushed about as well.

First the Jewish Council and the high priest questioned him. But Jesus said nothing. They repeated words that Jesus had said, accusing him of all kinds of things. But Jesus said nothing. Finally they said: 'Are you the Messiah, the son of the living God?'

'I am,' said Jesus.

'That's enough!' they cried. 'He has claimed to be God! Put him to death!'

And the soldiers mocked him and beat him.

Then they took him to Pilate, the Roman ruler. Pilate questioned him. Again Jesus said nothing.

At Passover, Pilate always freed one prisoner chosen by the crowds. He offered them a choice between Barabbas, a violent murderer, or Jesus.

'Shall I free Jesus, the King of the Jews?' asked Pilate.

'No!' roared the crowd. 'We have no king but Caesar! We want Barabbas! Barabbas! Barabbas!'

'But what shall I do with Jesus?' Pilate asked.

'Crucify him! Crucify him!' yelled the crowd, louder than ever.

So Pilate handed Jesus over to be nailed to a cross.

Episode 4: The death

The soldiers led Jesus away from Pilate into the courtyard. They began to mock him, bully him and beat him. They put a purple robe around him and a crown of thorns on his head. They spat on him and pretended to worship him. Jesus was forced to pick up his cross and carry it. When he fell, the soldiers grabbed a man from the crowd, a visitor to the city called Simon of Cyrene. He took Jesus' place, carrying the cross out to the area called Golgotha.

Then the nails were banged in – one, two, three, four. Jesus was raised high on the cross. The soldiers sat around and played dice to see if they could win his clothes, sometimes stopping to laugh at Jesus. People walked by. They stopped and said terrible things about Jesus. 'You saved others, get on with it, and save yourself!' said the chief priests and teachers.

Festivals Together (London: SPCK). Copyright © Sandra Millar 2012

Hours go by. Then the sky begins to go dark, very dark. At about three o'clock, Jesus cries out in a loud voice: 'My God, my God, why have you forsaken me?'

The people think he is calling Elijah. They try to give him wine on a sponge. Jesus gives a loud cry and dies.

At that very moment the curtain in the temple rips from top to bottom. One of the soldiers stares round in the gloom and says: 'For sure, this man is the Son of God.'

Then the women and some other friends come and take his body away. They lay him in a tomb, and a huge stone is rolled over.

It is over. Jesus is dead.

Festivals Together (London: SPCK). Copyright © Sandra Millar 2012

An alternative structure for Palm Sunday

This is for use when a procession is short and the service will take place inside the building. Everyone will need to have a palm cross, and some metal paper clips.

 ## WE GATHER

With blessing of palms (as in the main text) followed by a procession in or through the worship space.

We say sorry

This may be omitted.

 ## WE LISTEN

Either read as usual, or use the poem, 'Three Cheers for Jesus'* or use alternative passion drama, 'I'm a disciple, get me out of here!' (Additional resource: Palm Sunday 3, which follows this one).

 ## WE RESPOND

Use prayers in four sections, as below.

Section 1

Voice 1 Jesus gathered with his friends for a meal. (*Invite people to hold their palm cross.*) Lord God, thank you for the stories you told, the things you did, the words you said. Help us, your church, to remember well all that your life and death mean, and to live our lives serving other people.

Lord, in your mercy

All **hear our prayer.**

Section 2

Voice 2 Jesus was deserted by his friends and left alone. (*Invite people to make small huddles of three or four.*) Lord God, thank you that you call us to live in families and communities. We pray for our friends and for those we love, especially those who may be struggling with difficulties. Help us to be strong and faithful in helping others.

Lord, in your mercy

All **hear our prayer.**

*Peter Dainty, *The Electric Bible: Poems for Public Worship*, Stowmarket: Kevin Mayhew, 2003.

1

Section 3

Voice 3 Jesus was unjustly tried and found guilty. (*Invite people in pairs to make a long chain of metal paper clips to represent those who are being unfairly treated.*) Lord God, we pray for our world and especially those places where there is injustice. Give courage to those who are struggling to work for peace and speak out for truth. Strengthen all of us as we work to see your kingdom come.

Lord, in your mercy

All **hear our prayer.**

Section 4

Voice 4 Jesus died. (*Invite people to sit quietly, with one hand over their heart and their other hand over their eyes.*) Lord God, hear our prayers and help us to follow you.

All **Amen.**

We celebrate: Eucharist

 **WE GO OUT INTO THE WORLD**

Conclude as indicated in the main text.

Festivals Together (London: SPCK). Copyright © Sandra Millar 2012

'I'm a disciple, get me out of here!'

A re-telling of the Passion narrative

This script can be adapted and altered to suit. It is a good opportunity for young adults/teenagers to participate.

There are eight speaking parts. One person needs to be dressed in plain dark clothes for the last scene.

Each person carries a short stick with a card attached, bearing their name.

You will need some music suitable for the beginning of a game show.

You will also need some placards to prompt congregational participation and someone (or two) to encourage/lead the participation.

The characters enter as indicated and stand in a line centre stage, like contestants on a game show.

You will need a chair (to stand on) close by for the last scene.

Introducing the disciples

(*Each person walks forward carrying a name card on a stick. Theme music blares out – if possible from a TV game show or similar style.*)

TV show host   Well, it's time to meet our final contestants for this year's 'I'm a disciple, get me out of here!' You've had a chance to get to know the guys and gals over the past three years, as they've followed Jesus through the ups and downs of life, and now, as the going gets tough, we'll find out whether the tough get going as the pace hots up and the demands get stranger. Let's meet some of our final few.

Peter   Hi, I'm Peter, although the guys also know me as Simon. I used to be big in the fishing world, had a happy home with my wife's mother, kept an eye out on my little brother, but you know, I took a break. Followed this preacher about for a while . . . and now I'm ready to take the final challenge. I reckon I'll win – I've got the strength, got the character, and I'm pretty loyal. I'll still be standing at the end of the game!

(*After each introduction the person stands to one side of the 'stage' area.*)

John   Hi, I'm John – a bit of a mixture really . . . Most people know me as a dreamer, as a poet, even a performance poet – but when I get angry . . . then people had better look out. You might have read about me, my mum and my brother James yelling for our rights. We're not always popular with the others but I'm in with a good chance of being there at the end – quiet, determined, oh and a bit of a favourite, if you know what I mean.

1

Mary   I'm Mary – Mags to my friends, 'cos I come from Magdala. I'm the one who makes the front pages! If they can get my story they'll go wild! I've had a bit of a past, but I'm in recovery now, and I've been sticking close to my friends. This last week is going to be a challenge for me. I can be a bit emotional, and I don't really expect to win . . . but you have to give it a try.

Martha   I'm Martha – the guys love having me around, 'cos I'm a great cook. If there's a problem, I'll fix it – I'm fun, sociable and hard-working . . . but the last few weeks have been tough, and I've quietened down a lot. Not sure if I'll make it through . . .

Judas   Judas, Jude, that's me. Brave, bold and eager for action. The hard man of the group. I'm going to stick it out till the end . . . after all, we want to WIN! We want to see FREEDOM! And I'm the one to make it happen.

Thomas   I'm Tom, or Thomas, and I'm not really sure how I got into this group. I'm a bit hesitant, not sure if it's really my thing, but I'll give it a go. If it's real, if I can get my hands dirty as it were, I'll know where I am. I hope I'll stick it out . . . but it's fifty-fifty.

TV show host   You've met the guys – and now before we hear about the challenges, let's hear about the great event that began the week . . . it's procession time!

(*The disciples make their way down the church, waving banners and placards with words: 'Hosanna', etc. – the crowd join in.*)

Peter   This is great fun! We had to find our own donkey, sit Jesus on it, and then walk through a heaving mass of people down into Jerusalem. The people are going wild!

TV show host   Let's hear a bit of a replay of the action from the crowd.

Congregation   Hosanna, Hosanna! (*etc.*)

Peter   It was more like a party than a challenge – and we all survived . . . maybe it made us feel safe, as if we were heading straight for success. But then came the first real hurdle.

Judas   Yes, we were asked to find a room, and sort out the Passover meal. (*Remaining disciples make a tableau as if dining while Judas speaks.*) It was team work really – Martha and the girls rallied round with the food, while I and one of the boys set up the room. We created a really good atmosphere. Things were looking good – we were all there, laughing and chatting with Jesus, when it became serious. Jesus started talking about death and suffering, getting really heavy. Well, I don't mind a challenge – that's why I signed up – but it didn't seem right to me. I mean, the conditions were all wrong, not quite what I expected when I signed up, so . . .

TV show host   Judas became the first to say 'I'm a disciple, get me out of here!' – and left the supper, deciding to take matters into his own hands. It doesn't make it any easier for those who remain.

John   The next challenge was called 'In the garden'. I suppose we thought it might be a moonlit prayer meeting or something . . . but it wasn't that easy. We were asked simply to stay awake – no fighting, no talking, no miracles. Just to stay awake and wait with Jesus. Actually, only three of us decided to do this challenge – Peter, and me and James. We were pretty close to the action really. But it just got worse and worse.

Jesus was getting really upset. He was weeping and crying out, and me and James didn't know what to do.

And then we saw a crowd coming in – and Judas was with them.

'Oh, oh!' I said to James, 'I'm a disciple, but I'm out of here!' So I legged it – one or two tried to make a fight of it, chopping off an ear . . . but that wasn't what was wanted. Calm, stillness, acceptance – and we couldn't do it.

Peter   It was getting really tough now. We staggered off to the high priest's house. And the questioning and torture began. The challenge we faced was to stick with it, remain steadfast. But each of us had our own challenge – and I faced the 'Who do you know?' challenge. Girls kept asking me questions: Where are you from? Do you know him? You were his friend . . . and all I had to do was say yes . . . but I couldn't face it. I said no, I didn't know anything – and 'I'm a disciple, get me out of here!' I left, couldn't face any more.

Thomas   Not many left now. Perhaps a surprising group – the women, me, some others . . . and now we had to do 'The journey'. We had to walk with Jesus, watching him carry a cross. It was horrible. Whatever the Romans say, it's not entertainment! The crowd were yelling . . . and some were weeping and wailing . . .

TV show host   Here's a clip to remind you. (*Disciples hold placards up.*)

Congregation   Crucify, crucify!

Thomas   (*sobbing*) I couldn't face it, it was worse than my worst fears. So I slipped to the back of the crowd – get me out of here! – and one of the crew helped Jesus out, Simon of Cyrene. He should have been a disciple really – had more courage than any of us . . . and so all of us who thought we were winners were losers . . . and following a loser it seemed.

Martha   Not quite all. We girls were still there, walking, watching, but I kept wishing I wasn't. I wished one of the boys had made the final few. I felt so helpless – there was nothing I could do . . . but I just kept walking, walking. Thinking of all the things Jesus had said, muttering to myself, trying to stick it out.

TV show host   It seems to be getting worse . . . the conditions are extreme. Can any of them make it? Can any of them stay with Jesus until the end?

Mags   There were no words left, only silence. We couldn't ask to leave, not now.

Voice   (*reads Luke 23.44–49*)

Festivals Together (London: SPCK). Copyright © Sandra Millar 2012

(*The person wearing plain dark clothes climbs on to a chair, facing the back, arms wide; the two women fall at the foot . . . Lights dim.*

Then Jesus climbs down and Mags and Martha cradle him.)

Voice (*reads Luke 23.53–56, modified to begin: 'They took down the body of Jesus, wrapped it in linen cloth . . .'*)

Mags There were no winners at all that day.

Festivals Together (London: SPCK). Copyright © Sandra Millar 2012

Maundy Thursday

Food, feet and feelings

Maundy Thursday may not be an obvious occasion on which to offer all-age worship. Yet it is a vital festival in the church year, as we remember the pivotal events leading up to Jesus' death on Good Friday. There are some very dramatic stories, including the giving of bread and wine, the foot-washing, the foretelling of betrayal and denial and the struggle in the garden of Gethsemane. These are powerful stories, dealing with deep feelings, and the liturgies and traditions that have grown up for this day are also full of powerful drama and emotion. This may be why churches have not seen these as opportunities for the whole church family to share together. Yet because they offer a real possibility of experiencing the events rather than learning about them, they are also full of potential for all ages to be together.

This is one of the occasions when the physical space available and the numbers attending may well dictate the exact form that the worship can take. In a church where there is an easy transition from a hall to a worship space, then a liturgy taking place in and through a meal may be appropriate. For others it may be possible to move around the space in small groups, before gathering together for the last part of the service. These approaches work very well with smaller numbers, where the logistics are flexible. But even if physical movement is limited, there are suggestions here which allow the drama of movement and action to be explored.

There are two outlines offered, both with suggestions for incorporating the Eucharist. The first involves moving around the worship space in small groups. The second takes place around a meal.

Key lectionary readings

NB: Please see note on lectionary readings in 'How to use this book' (p. 13).

Lent and Holy Week is a season that requires the set lectionary readings for the day in a Church of England principal service.

Exodus 12.3–4, 11–14 'God's great Passover'
1 Corinthians 11.23–26 'Remembering for ever'
John 13.1–17 'Learning how to serve'

Preparation

Option 1

You will need to create four locations or stations around the edge of the worship space.

- *Location 1*: Set up a small low table (or a plank on bricks) and set it as if for a meal. Include a platter with pitta bread, a jug and a cup, some plates of herbs. Put cushions around, enough for six or so people. (The aim is to hint at a Passover scene, not to recreate a Passover meal.)

- *Location 2*: Place two large bowls on the floor with towels, spare towels to pick up and use. Jugs of water, chairs and kneelers may also be helpful. You will also need some pre-prepared foot shapes, and pens or markers.

- *Location 3*: A place with plenty of candles ready to light, a CD player with soft music. A small table with bread and wine or other eucharistic symbols.

- *Location 4*: Three or four garden seed trays (without holes!) filled with play sand, together with objects for creating a garden, e.g. small stones, cones, wood pieces, small dried grasses, etc. (see flower-arranging section in good craft shops).

At the front, you will need to create a prayer wall (e.g. using lining paper, a pinboard or notice board) or prayer tree. Have paper strips available for people to write on, and pens or markers to write with.

You will also need to have enough leaders for small groups of about six.

Option 2

You will need:

- a table set for the number of people and type of meal to be served
- a large candle
- bowls, jugs and towels for foot-washing.

If you plan to have a meal, see 'Practical notes for meal' on p. 47.

 # WE GATHER

Option 1

Meet people at the door or in the narthex. As soon as six people have arrived, they form a group and set off with a leader. As the group is assembled, the leader formally starts the journey through the space.

Voice The Lord be with you

All of group **and also with you.**

Groups of six set off at intervals, allowing time for groups to move around the four locations. Make sure there are waiting areas between stages.

Location 1

The group sits around the table. Invite one person to read Exodus 12.3–4, 11–14.

Remind people that the meal that Jesus attended was a Passover meal. Passover has been celebrated by Jewish people for thousands of years.

Invite the group to place their hands on the table, then give thanks to God for his faithfulness over many years.

Read this short litany:

Leader	Faithful God, For those who long for freedom
All	**we pray this morning/night.**
Leader	For those escaping from injustice and oppression
All	**we pray this morning/night.**
Leader	For those forced to move through hunger and famine
All	**we pray this morning/night.**
Leader	For those remembering special times and places
All	**we pray this morning/night.**
Leader	For God's people keeping faith and holding hope
All	**we pray this morning/night.**
Leader	For God's faithful love in this place and in our lives
All	**we pray this morning/night.**

Location 2

As the group arrives at the foot-washing location, invite someone to read John 13.1–17.

Leader	'This is our God, the Servant King' (*read chorus from this hymn or sing quietly*).
All	**He calls us now to follow him.**
Leader	Lord, Jesus Christ, help us now to follow you, and as our feet are washed, give us the courage to receive help from others and the confidence to serve.
All	**Amen.**

Encourage people to wash one another's feet.

Then invite each person in the group to pick up a footprint, write a short prayer on it if they want, and start to make a trail around the foot-washing space. As each footprint is laid, it is a prayer for our own commitment to serve others.

Location 3

Invite the group to sit quietly.

Then one person reads from 1 Corinthians 11.23–36. Invite people to listen as music plays, e.g. Margaret Rizza, Taizé or similar, and to light a candle as a sign of their prayers.

Location 4

Invite the group to sit in ones and twos with a sand garden and create their own garden as they listen to the reading. Invite them to remember all that Jesus did for us, and also pray for those who are in need this night.

Read from Luke 22.39–45.

Then the leader brings the time to an end with these or similar words:

Leader   Be with all who are alone this night, keep us in our times of struggle,
And help us to do all that you ask of us. Amen.

Location 5

When a group has moved through all four locations, they go to sit in the body of the church.

While waiting for all the groups to finish, invite people to write or draw their prayers on the strips of paper, which can either be tied to the branches of the tree or placed on the prayer wall.

When everyone is in the central space, share the peace together.

A hymn is sung or music played, during which the bread and wine are brought forward and children and young people set the altar.

Then invite everyone to stand around the altar.

Eucharistic prayer

After the Eucharist, let silence fall before saying:

Minister   Lord Jesus,
we thank you that you gave us bread and wine
so we might remember your story of love;
we thank you that you washed the disciples'
feet
so we might learn to show love to others.
Help us to stay close to you
and live as your followers day by day,
through Jesus Christ our Lord.
Amen.

(Silence. NB: drama and atmosphere are vital at this point.)

Leader   And it was night.

Stripping of the altar

The altar cloths and linens are removed, together with any ornaments in the sanctuary area, in silence. Use children to help as appropriate. Finally the lights are lowered and all but one candle extinguished.

Voice   When the disciples had sung a hymn they went out to the Mount of Olives. Jesus prayed to the Father, 'If it is possible, take this cup of suffering from me.' He said to his disciples, 'How is it that you were not able to keep this

watch with me one hour? The hour has come for the Son of Man to be handed over to the power of sinful people. Come, let us go.'
(Pause.)
Christ was obedient unto death. Go in his peace.

The people leave as quietly as possible.[1]

Alternative to Option 1

If you are unable to create four locations or divide people into small groups, this alternative involves the whole congregation moving through the space.

Start the service by gathering everyone together towards the back of the church and listen to the Exodus reading and prayer.

Then move towards the front rows to do the foot-washing; then read John 13.1–17.

Invite people to find a quiet space to think about Jesus being alone. They could sit still, or sit or lie down on the floor.

Then light candles as part of the intercessions.

Continue as above from the peace.

Option 2[2]

This is based around a meal.

 # WE GATHER

If a meal, make sure everyone is seated and ready.

Leader   The Lord be with you
All   **and also with you.**
Voice   They gathered in an upper room to share a meal. We remember them tonight.
(Light the large candle and place in middle of table.)
Voice   Come, Lord Jesus, take your rightful place as host at this, your table.

Collect for the day or this prayer

NB: Please see note on the collect or prayer for the day in 'How to use this book' (p. 14).

Minister   Loving God, whose Son showed us how to serve,
who gave us bread and wine,
so we could remember him always,
help us, your people, to accept these gifts

and follow him day by day,
through Jesus Christ our Lord.

All   **Amen.**

WE LISTEN

Reading(s)

While people eat starters/nibbles, these readings are read in a straightforward way:

Exodus 12.3–4, 11–14
1 Corinthians 11.23–26
John 13.1–17 (use a contemporary version such as *The Message*)

Talk

This should be a brief reflection based on a real anecdote or using the following story.

> We do funny things in the church, making ordinary things like eating into solemn rituals.
>
> A true story: Many years ago someone was in India on a mission trip and one evening, walking back from a visit, she stepped into an open sewer: not unusual in India, but still horrible.
>
> When the group got back to their base, a seven-year-old boy from the group offered to wash the feet of the woman who had stepped in the sewer. She sat on a stool and they chatted together while he washed off all the smell and gunk of the sewer. It was very moving.
>
> When the boy had had finished he said: 'And now I'm going to do a Christian foot-washing.'
>
> The woman was puzzled. She thought that what he had just done was the most Christian foot-washing she had ever experienced. So she asked: 'What's the difference between what you have just done and a Christian foot-washing, then?'
>
> He thought for a moment and then said: 'You don't use soap and a towel in a Christian foot-washing.'
>
> He then proceeded to get a bowl of clean water and dribble it over her feet!
>
> She realized that he thought foot-washing was the kind of sanitized ritual done on Maundy Thursday.
>
> We have a habit in church of making ordinary things like washing dirty feet into rituals.

Reflect on what the Last Supper was really like, compared with paintings and images: probably like a lot of gatherings with family and friends – chatting, some laughing, a bit of annoyance from time to time. Even the saddest family gatherings often end up like this; think of the meal after a funeral. Sooner or later someone says: 'Do you remember when . . . ?' Then everyone starts talking again.

> The meal that Jesus and his disciples shared together was a Passover meal, a time to remember and celebrate God's action in Jewish history. There was probably tension and doubt as well as normality: but slowly the mood changed as Jesus did things differently and gave us something special to do to remember his story, his action in our lives and history. There is so much to remember tonight.

Remind people that during the evening they will enact the foot-washing, then share a meal, then have bread and wine, and slowly move towards the long night of agony as Jesus faced the cross. Encourage people to choose one thing to think about to help them remember: maybe the bread, maybe the towel and the bowl, maybe the jug of wine. Invite them to treasure this in the back of their minds as the sharing continues.

WE RESPOND

Creed or statement of faith

Prayer for foot-washing

Voice   'This is our God, the Servant King'.

All   **He calls us now to follow him.**

Voice   Lord, Jesus Christ, help us now to follow you,
          and as our feet are washed,
          give us the courage to receive help from others
          and the confidence to serve the world.

All   **Amen.**

Foot-washing

Do this according to local practice or, ideally, if doing it at a meal, it can be done more informally; encourage children to have their feet washed and to wash others. Encourage conversation and eating to go on, and create a sense of normality.

When everyone who wishes has had their feet washed:

Voice   Loving God,
          Jesus taught us that what we do for people in need

is like doing things for him.
Help us to serve others just as he was the servant of all.

All **Amen.**

Serve main course and as it draws to a close invite people to pray.

Choose people around the table to read different sections, using these or similar words.

Prayers

Each section to be read by a different voice.

Voice 1 Father, on this, the night he was betrayed, your Son Jesus Christ washed his disciples' feet. Help us to follow his example of love and service in humility.

All **Lord, in your mercy, hear our prayer.**

Voice 2 We pray for the mission of your Church, and ask that you help us to learn from each other and work together for the spread of the good news as you unite us in love.

All **Lord, in your mercy, hear our prayer.**

Voice 3 On this night, Jesus commanded them to love, but suffered rejection himself.

We pray for the rejected and unloved, the outcast and refugee, and ask that we be filled with your love for others.

All **Lord, in your mercy, hear our prayer.**

Voice 4 On this night, Jesus reminded them that if the world hated them it hated him first. We pray for those who are persecuted for their faith, and for all who live in fear of violence and injustice. Give us your peace and help us to be peacemakers.

All **Lord, in your mercy, hear our prayer.**

The peace

Minister Jesus says: 'Peace I leave with you; my peace I give to you.
Do not let your hearts be troubled, neither let them be afraid.'
The peace of the Lord be always with you

All **and also with you.**[3]

Minister Let us offer one another a sign of peace. (*Share the peace around the table.*)

If a meal, serve dessert, then clear tables. After dessert – bread and wine are brought out and an appropriate part of the table is prepared.

Preparation of gifts

Minister or other voice As we share bread and wine in the Eucharist,
we are with our crucified and risen Lord.
We know that it was not only our ancestors,
but we who were redeemed
and brought from slavery to freedom,
from sadness to celebration.
We know that as he was with them in the upper room
so our Lord is here with us now.

All **He is with us now.**[4]

Eucharistic prayer – using appropriate preface

Service continues as normal Eucharist through to distribution.

Suggestion: if seated around a table, people could pass the elements from one to another or those administering communion could walk around the table.

When distribution is finished, say a prayer in these or similar words:

Leader Lord Jesus,
we thank you that you gave us bread and wine
so we might remember your story of love;
we thank you that you washed the disciples' feet
so we might learn to show love to others.
Help us to stay close to you
and live as your followers day by day,
through Jesus Christ our Lord.
Amen.

(*Silence. NB: drama and atmosphere are vital at this point.*)

Leader And it was night.

Blow out any candles except the large one. Lower the lights if possible. Invite a child to carry the single candle. Move in silence to the sanctuary. The single candle is placed on the altar.

When everyone is in place, proceed with the stripping of the altar.

Stripping of the altar

The altar cloths and linens are removed, together with any ornaments in the sanctuary area, in silence.

Voice   When the disciples had sung a hymn they went out to the Mount of Olives. Jesus prayed to the Father, 'If it is possible, take this cup of suffering from me.' He said to his disciples, 'How is it that you were not able to keep this watch with me one hour? The hour has come for the Son of Man to be handed over to the power of sinful men. Come, let us go.'
(*Pause.*)

 ## WE GO OUT

Voice   Christ was obedient unto death.
Go in his peace.[4]

Leave as quietly as is practical.

NB: Some churches create a place to watch and pray. It may be appropriate to create a station based on material designed for schoolchildren, e.g. *Experience Easter* (Jumping Fish, 2007) or similar idea.

Practical notes for meal

This is not a Passover, just a family meal. A simple menu might be:

- starters: pitta bread, houmous and olives

- main: shepherd's pie (made with either mince or a vegetarian alternative such as Quorn) with salad

- dessert: cheesecake or similar, or fruit salad

Experience has shown that it is better to have a menu and ask people to provide that item for six than to have a bring-and-share.

It is useful to give people a full service sheet and to give instructions at the beginning about times for silence, etc. It is particularly important to encourage silence at the end – maybe suggest that people stay for a while at an appropriate place in church, leaving materials there for children and adults to create a response, e.g. the sand gardens or the prayer wall.

It should be treated as a family meal and kept as natural as possible. The introduction of liturgy is then very dramatic. It allows people to experience the powerful shift of mood that happens as we prepare for Good Friday.

Notes

1 *Common Worship: Times and Seasons*, London: Church House Publishing, 2006, p. 304, adapted.
2 Adapted from Sandra Millar, *Resourcing Easter*, Gloucester: Jumping Fish, 2008.
3 *New Patterns for Worship*, London: Church House Publishing, 2008, p. 273, H9.
4 *Times and Seasons*, p. 300, adapted.

Good Friday

Serious stillness

Good Friday is always a public holiday in the United Kingdom, regardless of where Easter and school holidays fall. This means it is increasingly an opportunity for churches to engage with a range of ages. However, Good Friday presents particular challenges. The profoundly moving solemn liturgies use silence, sometimes music, profound reflections and complex language to help explore the deepest of Christian mysteries. These things are not the easiest for younger people to engage with – and can also be difficult for those who face physical challenges. Yet the story concerns the ultimate universal truth that Christians celebrate: that God so loved the world that he gave his only-begotten Son, so that everyone who believes in him should not perish but have everlasting life. Everyone includes all ages.

This worship outline is offered as a way of helping all ages share together in the story of Good Friday, and includes times of silence and stillness as well as the opportunity to respond creatively. Remember that children are often deeply engaged by Taizé and similar worship involving candles, images and chants, which gives them an opportunity to encounter faith rather than be educated or entertained by stories.

You might like to begin or end the worship by showing a film such as *Miracle Maker*.

Key readings

See 'Additional resource: Good Friday' at the end of this outline (pp. 51–3).

Preparation

You will need

- Five large candles

- Five 3- to 5-metre lengths of fabric in white, indigo or navy, purple, red and black
- Lengths of wool in the same colours, cut long enough to go round a wrist twice (to plait and tie), enough for each person to have a set
- Scented fabric rose petals (or real petals)
- Gold confetti
- Dark brown/grey strips of thin card
- Red paper and scissors, or red heart shapes
- Clear glass pebbles, or stones
- Map of the world
- Pieces of gold thread about 6 cm in length

To make scented rose petals: separate the petals from some silk roses. Soak these for at least two hours in water with an essential oil added. Remove from the water and allow to dry.

WE GATHER

Hand out the short pieces of coloured wool to everyone.

As is traditional for Good Friday, begin in silence.

Voice   For God so loved the world, that he gave his only Son, so that everyone who believes in him might live.

Light five large candles on the altar.

Collect for the day or this prayer

NB: Please see note on the collect or prayer for the day in 'How to use this book' (p. 14).

Voice   Eternal God,
in the cross of Jesus
we see the cost of our sin
and the depth of your love:

in humble hope and fear
may we place at his feet
all that we have and all that we are,
through Jesus Christ our Lord.[1]

All **Amen.**

Part 1

Place a long length of white fabric over the altar or in another significant space.

Wonder about the colour white, which is the colour of holiness and perfection. Say something similar to:

> It is the colour of peace, and the colour of new beginnings. It is the place we start our Good Friday journey as we remember Jesus.
>
> Jesus did so many good things and taught so many true things. He healed people, brought life, changed tears to laughing, answered some questions and provoked many more.
>
> He was perfect and pure and holy.
>
> Hear the words of the prophet Isaiah from 500 years before Jesus' time.

Read Isaiah 53.4–6, 11, if not reading whole chapter, from CEV or similar. (See 'Additional resource: Good Friday' at the end of this outline (pp. 51–3) for suggested script for all readings.)

Extinguish first candle.

Then invite people to hold the length of white wool and remember something Jesus did in his life and simply say thank you.

End with a simple gathering prayer, e.g.

Minister Loving God, we thank you for Jesus,
for all we see in him of your life and love.
You gave your life that we might live.
Lord, in your mercy

All **hear our prayer.**

Either sing a hymn or play a short piece of music.

Part 2

Place a length of indigo/dark blue fabric next to the white fabric.

Wonder about indigo, and how dark colours make us think about sadness and injustice, about times in our lives and in our world when things go wrong. Say something similar to:

Things are beginning to go wrong on our Good Friday journey as Jesus prays in the garden.

One of his friends, Judas, betrays him. Others simply run away. Those who have heard him teach in public all day long, come in darkness to arrest him. In the darkness, they arrest the one who is light.

Read John 18.1–11 (or other Gospel or 'Betrayed' in 'Additional Resource: Good Friday', which follows this outline (p. 52).

Extinguish second candle.

Invite people to begin to tie the dark wool to the white.

Then invite people to come forward to collect real or fabric petals and drop into the font or a large bowl of water. Rose petals look a bit like tear shapes so make a good symbol for times of sadness.

When everyone has done this, pray a short gathering prayer ending as in Part 1.

Either sing a hymn or play a short piece of music.

Part 3

Place a length of purple fabric next.

Wonder about why purple appears – a rich colour, colour of kings and leaders. Say something similar to:

> All through Lent the Church has been decorated in purple as we thought about what kind of king Jesus would be – not a king ruling with power and might, but the Servant King. Pilate talked to him about what kind of king he was, and Jesus was clear that he is not a king like those in this world. As he went from trial to trial, the soldiers and onlookers mocked him, laughing at the things he said. Then it became worse as they whipped him and dressed him up as if he were a king – in a purple robe and with a crown of thorns.

Read from John 19.1–7 or 'Not a king' in 'Additional resource: Good Friday', which follows this outline (p. 52).

Extinguish third candle.

Invite people to tie the purple thread to the white and indigo.

Then weave the brown/grey strips into a circle to represent the crown of thorns. While this is happening encourage people to talk together quietly about what Good Friday means to them.

If you use technology you could project some images of Jesus.

Alternatively invite people to come forward and scatter gold confetti crowns onto the fabric as they pray. End this time with a gathering prayer as in Part 1. Either sing a hymn or play a short piece of music.

Part 4

Place red fabric next to the other colours.

Say something similar to:

> Red is a very special colour. It is the colour of danger, the colour that warns us that things are not safe, tells us to stop and take note. It's the colour we think of when we think of anger – seeing red.
>
> But red is also the colour of love, and the colour of life. We might feel angry when we think of what is happening to Jesus, who is so good and pure and holy. We might feel love for him, when we realize how much he loves us. We might simply wonder at how his life is ending.

Read from Mark 15.21–32 or 'On the cross' in 'Additional resource: Good Friday', which follows this outline (p. 53).

Extinguish fourth candle.

Invite people to tie red thread to the others. Either invite people to cut out four heart shapes from red paper, or hand out pre-cut hearts.

Voice   For God so loved the world he gave his only son.

        (After each section of the prayers invite people to go and place a heart as indicated.)

Voice   On this Good Friday, we pray for God's Church, asking that God will help us all to follow him and share the message of his love with others.

        (Place a heart near the font.)

Voice   On this Good Friday, we pray for God's world, where there is so much hurt, asking that through Jesus' death and his new life people will find peace in him.

        (Place a heart on a map of the world in an appropriate place.)

Voice   On this Good Friday, we pray for our community, our homes and our families, asking God to help us show love to all those around us.

        (Place a heart near to the door.)

Voice   On this Good Friday, we pray for all those who are feeling alone or afraid, and who are finding life very difficult for whatever reason.

        (Place a heart at the foot of the cross or on the altar. When everyone has returned to their seat:)

Voice   On this Good Friday, we trust in your love that always hears our prayers.
    Amen.

Either sing a hymn or play a short piece of music.

Part 5

Place colour black next to all the other colours.

Say something similar to:

> Black is the colour that often reminds us of complete sadness, of death, of things being finished and over. That is how we end this day, remembering that Jesus died.

Read Mark 15.33–41 or 'It's over' in 'Additional resource: Good Friday', which follows this outline. (p. 53).

Extinguish last candle.

Invite people to tie the black thread, and then plait their five colours into a bracelet.

Invite people to come and place clear glass pebbles onto the fabrics (or at the foot of the cross) as they remember this final moment of Jesus.

Gather prayers together in these or similar words:

Voice   Lord, we have heard your story. We remember your love for us. Be with us as we wait for the good news of Easter.
    Amen.

Final hymn/music

 WE GO OUT

Leave in silence, and give people a small gold thread as they leave, as a hint that resurrection is coming.

Note

1 *Common Worship: Additional Collects*, London: Church House Publishing, 2004, p. 15.

Some readings

These are story texts based on selected readings for Good Friday.

Based on Isaiah 53

Long ago
Long before Jesus was born
A prophet spoke
Spoke of a time that was to come, things that were to happen,
A person that would come to help,
To help and to save people who were lost,
Who were lost like sheep, lost and far from God,
Choosing to do wrong, not right; choosing their own way, not God's way.

But he wouldn't be a handsome hero, and he wouldn't be a mighty warrior,
He wouldn't be cheered by crowds and adored by millions.
Nobody, but nobody, would want to be his friend.
Instead, everybody, but everybody would laugh at him,
Would laugh and jeer and mock and tease.
He would be a nobody.

But this is the man,
This is the man who will take the pain for the lost,
Who will lead us home and keep us safe.
He will be beaten, beaten and not cry out;
He will be like a lamb quietly going to die,
He will go to die without a sound,
He will be accused without reason, without reason sent to die.
He will be cut off from the land of the living,
He will die like a poor man, alone and without friends,
He will be buried with the wicked,
Though nothing wicked had been in his heart or on his lips.
This is the one,
This is the one who will turn darkness into light,
And his light will lead us home;
This is the one.

Long ago,
Long ago the prophet said
'Wait. For this one will come.'

Betrayed (John 18.1–11 and elsewhere)

They were in the garden, waiting and hoping. Jesus was praying. His friends were sleeping.

The calm was broken, the silence destroyed as a crowd of soldiers pushed and shoved into the darkness. The torches and the lanterns flashed through the trees, and the beam sought out the one they were looking for. Into the space stepped Jesus. Into the space stepped Judas.

Jesus spoke: 'Who do you want?'

And Judas leaned towards him, hugged him, kissed him. 'You. They want you.'

Judas turned to the soldier and said: 'This is the one.'

And Jesus said: 'I am he.'

So they grabbed him and took him away. But he didn't fight and he didn't struggle . . . though some of the others did.

Not a king (John 18.28—19.16 and elsewhere)

Early in the morning, Jesus was taken to Pilate's place. By now it was Passover.

Pilate asked them what Jesus was supposed to have done.

'He says he is a king,' the religious leaders said.

'Deal with it,' said Pilate.

'We're not allowed to put anyone to death,' they replied.

So Pilate had Jesus brought inside and began to ask him questions. Over and over, again and again, he tried to get Jesus to say he was a king. But Jesus kept pointing Pilate to the truth, the truth that his kingdom is not of this world.

Then Jesus was whipped and mocked. Soldiers put a crown of thorns on his head and a purple robe on his shoulders, dressed him up like a king. They laughed and joked at the man who might have said he was a king.

Pilate tried again. He brought Jesus out, wearing the robe and the crown. All the religious leaders, the soldiers and the people called out, 'Crucify him! Crucify him! We have no king but Caesar!'

Pilate tried to get them to choose Barabbas to die and Jesus to live. But the crowds roared and cheered for Barabbas to live. So Jesus was sentenced to death.

On the cross (Mark 15.21–32 and elsewhere)

It was a long walk out to Golgotha, the place of the skull, a long walk for a beaten man carrying a cross. He stumbled and fell, so they grabbed a man from the crowd, a man called Simon from Cyrene, there with his sons. They made him carry the cross.

On the hillside they nailed Jesus to the cross. They raised him high among the others; then the soldiers sat around, drinking and gambling, gambling for Jesus' clothes. Over Jesus' head there was a sign saying: 'The king of the Jews'.

People passed by, shook their heads, pointed their fingers, laughed at Jesus. 'Who's going to save you now?' they said. 'If you can do so much, then get yourself off that cross.'

All around on every side, strangers, criminals, religious leaders, soldiers, all around they mocked Jesus. And his friends had run away . . . except for the women.

It's over (Mark 15.33–47 and elsewhere)

It was noon and darkness fell over all the land, not just for one hour, not for two, but for three long hours as Jesus struggled on the cross.

Then he gave a loud cry: 'Eloi, Eloi, lama sabachthani!' This means: 'My God, my God, why have you left me?'

But people didn't understand him, they thought he was calling for Elijah. They tried to give him sour wine to drink, while they waited to see if he would come down from the cross.

But then Jesus gave a loud cry and . . . and the loud cry was his last breath. At that exact moment the temple curtain ripped in two, the earth shook, and those around shook too. One of the soldiers suddenly said: 'For sure, this man was the Son of God.'

Then the women, who had been watching, waiting, weeping, came close. The soldiers took down Jesus' body from the cross and gave it to the women. A rich man called Joseph of Arimathea had been to see Pilate and asked if he could bury Jesus, and Pilate gave permission – but only after he made sure that Jesus was dead.

Jesus was wrapped in a linen cloth, and laid in the tomb, which was carved from the rocks. A stone was rolled against the door.

Jesus was dead.

Festivals Together (London: SPCK). Copyright © Sandra Millar 2012

Easter Vigil

Light in the dark

The Easter Vigil may be held on Saturday evening, or very early on Sunday morning. It is one of the great treasures in the Church's store of worship, and yet is rarely seen in terms of an event which can engage children and those on the edge of the Church. The dramatic elements draw on deep archetypes that speak across traditions and cut through intellectual comprehension to create real moments of astonishment. This service has the 'wow' factor!

The biggest obstacle to making it inclusive of younger people is often time – it needs to begin at sunset and, if Easter is at mid–late April, then this may mean a start time of 8.00 or even 8.30 p.m. The service itself will last around seventy-five minutes if you include a Eucharist (which can be deferred until Easter Day) but, because of the variety and the drama, this is not necessarily a problem for children, except that if it becomes very late little ones become fractious. Dawn timings equally present challenges – perhaps at the other end of the age spectrum; if you have rheumatoid arthritis, getting out of the house very early is often difficult.

However, if you can overcome the time problems, then this service is truly special. It involves movement, fire, darkness, noise, silence, water, laughter. The liturgy tells the whole story of God's saving love at work from the creation of the world through to the new life in Jesus, and also gives every Christian an opportunity to renew his or her own commitment as a disciple. It is a truly multi-sensory, multi-level experience of the amazing revelation that Jesus is alive – good news for everyone.

Preparation

NB: The notes and guidance in *Common Worship: Times and Seasons*, pp. 324–7, are very helpful. This outline is based around Pattern B.

You will need to set a bonfire (which represents the new light of Easter and also suggests the fire Jesus lit on the beach at one of the resurrection appearances), and to have rehearsed the mechanics of lighting the Easter candle from the fire (powerful symbolism is wiped out in a moment when a passing server sighs and the candle goes out!).

Think about the practicalities of having readings in semi-darkness. (The drama is lost if the lights go on suddenly, or a stage whisper says: 'How am I meant to read this?' This is the voice of experience speaking.) Brief organists and bell-ringers and provide lots of loud-noise equipment. If you are using fireworks, make sure you do so safely.

You will need

- A paschal/Easter candle (a very large candle, which represents the light of the risen Christ)
- A bonfire
- A taper
- Enough candles for everyone to hold one
- Everyday objects and children's instruments, e.g. saucepan lids, car keys, tambourines, maracas, castanets, rattles
- The font open and filled with water
- Fireworks

WE GATHER

Begin by gathering everyone in either the church or the church hall if it is adjacent. Take a few moments to explain the logistics and any safety procedures. The building should be in near darkness, and if candles are used they should not be lit from the Easter fire but in the usual way from matches or a taper.

The vigil

Minister	This is a special night. It is the night when the Church remembers that Jesus came from death to life. Down the ages and across the world Christians gather together to wait, and to pray. As we wait let's listen to the awesome story of all that God has done through the ages. Let's remember together how much God loves his world. Let's wait for the good news of Jesus to come and let's pray that we might be thrilled once more as we hear the message.

 # WE LISTEN

Readings

NB: Specific versions are recommended here to give variety and accessibility.

First reading: Genesis 1

Read from *The Lion Storyteller Bible*. Add sound effects as appropriate

OR read 'God's Week' from *The Electric Bible*.

Second reading: Exodus 14

Read from *The Big Bible Story Book* – 'A meal to remember and crossing the Red Sea'.

Third reading: Ezekiel 37

Read from *The Big Bible Story Book* – 'Ezekiel and God'.

(It is important to ensure these are read well, with real drama.)

When the readings are finished, everyone moves outside to gather round the Easter fire which is now lit. Make sure that the mechanics have been worked out with someone present to light the fire.

The leader prays using the appropriate prayers and including:

Leader	Christ yesterday and today, the beginning and the end, Alpha and Omega, all time belongs to him, and all ages; to him be glory and power, through every age and for ever.
All	**Amen.**[1]

(If the candle is marked with five nails this happens at this point. Please see notes in *Common Worship: Times and Seasons* for more information.)

 # WE RESPOND

Invite the people to renew the promises made at baptism as the Easter candle is lit from a taper taken from the new fire.

Minister	May the light of Christ, rising in glory, banish all darkness from our hearts and minds.[2]
	(*Then everyone processes into the church following the candle and the ministers. The person carrying the candle stops three times, saying:*)
Voice	The light of Christ
All	**Thanks be to God!**[3]
	(*Getting louder each time.*)

Light all the candles and place the Easter candle on a stand.

The minister sings the first part of the Exsultet.[4] (Suggestion: sing the first part and then read – make sure it is read very well; it has drama and rhythm and the language is not overly complex.)

If you decide to use the response 'Glory to you for ever', this could be accompanied by simple actions: 'Glory': (raise right hand with palm flat and open), 'for ever' (then lower slowly, keeping the hand forward).

Alternatively, use the shorter responsive version, during which the response can be accompanied by a rhythm tapped out on a drum or similar instrument.

Leader	Choirs of angels, stars and planets:
All	**all God's people sing and dance.**
Leader	All creation, Church of God:
All	**all God's people sing and dance.**
Leader	We praise you Lord of life and death: we glorify your name:

All	**all God's people sing and dance.**
Leader	This is the night you set us free, bringing us home in love; holy night, when you led your people through the fearsome sea:
All	**all God's people sing and dance.**
Leader	This is the night you brought your Son through the doors of death; O holy night, when death takes flight and hope is born again:
All	**all God's people sing and dance.**
Leader	This is the night our tears of sadness turn to shouts of joy; holy night, when the choirs of earth sing the songs of heaven:
All	**all God's people sing and dance.**
Leader	This is the night when Christ our Light makes the darkness bright:
All	**all God's people sing and dance.**
Leader	Christ is the life that knows no end. Christ is the love that burns within. Christ is the peace that floods the world. Christ is the Lord who reigns on high.
All	**All God's people sing and dance. Amen.[5]**
Minister	Alleluia! Christ is risen!
All	**He is risen indeed! Alleluia! Alleluia! Alleluia![6]**

This is accompanied by loud noise, cymbals, bells, organ, etc. Encourage people to use everyday objects and children's instruments, e.g. saucepan lids, car keys, tambourines, maracas, castanets, rattles.

A short song could be sung, e.g. 'God's not dead, no! he is alive'.

The Gloria

Suggestion: use the traditional Peruvian Gloria with responses.[7]

During this time all the church candles are lit, and the people's candles are blown out as the lights are put on.

Prayer for the day

Leader	God of glory, by the raising of your Son you have broken the chains of death and hell: fill your Church with faith and hope; for a new day has dawned and the way to life stands open in our Saviour Jesus Christ.
All	**Amen.[8]**

Readings

If you are using the New Testament reading from Romans, read from a contemporary version.

The Gospel could be announced with a fanfare.

This is one of the best occasions for the Gospel to be proclaimed from memory. It can be started on the chancel steps, and then the gospeller can move through the church making eye contact as the amazing story is told.

'This is the Gospel of the Lord' (repeat three times with growing emphasis). Encourage more noise.

The congregation all move to gather around the font.

The water is blessed, and if the response 'Saving God, give us life' is used, it can be said by a child or young person.

When the water is blessed, invite everyone to affirm their faith using an authorized creed or affirmation of faith.[9]

Then either sprinkle everyone with water – make this informal and enjoyable – or invite everyone to go and sign themselves with the cross from the water.

The service continues with the peace, and the Eucharist if being celebrated as part of the vigil.

 # WE GO OUT

If not a Eucharist, then continue with the dismissal and blessing after the peace, and go outside for fireworks!

Notes

1 *Common Worship: Times and Seasons,* London: Church House Publishing, 2006, p. 335.
2 *Times and Seasons,* p. 335.
3 *Times and Seasons,* p. 335.
4 *Times and Seasons,* p. 336.
5 *Times and Seasons,* p. 413.
6 *Times and Seasons,* p. 418.
7 *Complete Anglican Hymns Old and New,* Stowmarket: Kevin Mayhew, 1976, 966.
8 *Times and Seasons,* p. 360.
9 For example, E6 from *New Patterns for Worship,* London: Church House Publishing, 2008, p. 163.

Easter Sunday

The first time ever

Easter Sunday should be the most joyful event in the church year. Our churches are at their best on Easter Sunday, with glorious flowers and, where used, wonderful vestments. In the past churchgoers would wear their best – hence the tradition of the Easter bonnet, which may be worth reviving. Think of how much trouble goes into organizing a memorable celebration – as when the local team wins the FA Cup or for a particularly special party – and try to capture some of that energy and atmosphere. Much of this will come through the way the service is led, which means planning, preparation and direction are crucial.

Key lectionary readings

NB: Please see note on lectionary readings in 'How to use this book' (p. 13).

Easter is a season that requires the set lectionary readings for the day in a Church of England principal service.

Isaiah 65.17–25 'A whole new world'
Psalm 118.14–24 'Songs of victory'
Acts 10.34–43 'Have I got news for you'
Luke 24.1–12 OR John 20.1–18 'The first and only time'

Preparation

The previous week you will need to ask people if there is anything they will be doing for the first time during the next week, and if they are willing to come back next Sunday and tell us about it. (This is a feature idea from BBC Radio 2's *Big Breakfast Show*.) If this is not possible, there is an alternative way of beginning the talk.

You will need

- Baskets of party poppers, balloons, mini-eggs, mini-chicks, daffodils, etc.

- A basket of chocolate eggs or a large egg; broken egg shells; some tiny mini-eggs (ideally real objects, but if not use pictures)

- Two carrier bags – one filled with items such as food rubbish, a used tea towel, some sticking plasters, and broken things; the other with red confetti hearts

- Items for the five prayer stations: print-outs of prayer themes; fabric butterflies; (a picture of) a chrysalis; large stones, sticky notes or small pieces of paper; a bowl of eggs (real!), a bowl of mini-eggs – enough for everyone – with something for those who can't eat chocolate; daffodils in vase, clean plate

- An Easter garden. This will usually have been created in an appropriate space in church and will represent the garden tomb with the stone rolled away. Sometimes the cross(es) are also included. It is an activity often done by children and families during Easter Saturday, or by the church flower arrangers

- Angel-shaped pieces of paper, pencils

 ## WE GATHER

As people arrive and take their seats, various people walk about carrying baskets with balloons, party poppers, mini-eggs, mini-chicks, daffodils, etc. which they give away. Those holding the baskets greet people, saying: 'Alleluia! Christ is risen!'

Opening hymn

Informal welcome

Explain that Easter is the greatest festival in the Church – and when we celebrate we have parties and presents! That's why we've been giving away things – to remind ourselves that we have an amazing, generous God of surprises. In a moment we are going to declare the biggest surprise of all – so when you are ready, raise a huge shout.

After a short time invite everyone to join together:

Minister	Alleluia! Christ is risen!
All	**He is risen indeed! Alleluia!**[1]

We say sorry

Minister	Jesus is risen and all that is wrong can be made right. Let's be quiet for a moment and, as we look at each of these symbols, ask God to come close to us with his love and forgiveness.

Symbols could be held up or images projected onto a screen.

Invite people to look at the symbol as it is held up, then look down as the words are said. Use different voices for each section, including children.

Hold up a very large Easter egg or a basket with lots of smaller eggs.

Voice	Lord God, sometimes we are greedy and want to keep everything to ourselves. Forgive us for our selfishness. Lord, have mercy.
All	**Lord, have mercy.**
	(*Hold up some broken egg shells.*)
Voice	Lord God, sometimes we spoil things that are precious, the world and its people. Forgive us for our hatred. Christ, have mercy.
All	**Christ, have mercy.**
	(*Hold up some mini-eggs.*)
Voice	Lord God, sometimes we ignore or ridicule those who seem unimportant to us.

	Forgive us for our prejudice. Lord, have mercy.
All	**Lord, have mercy.**
Minister	May the Father of all mercies cleanse *us* from *our* sins, and restore *us* in his image to the praise and glory of his name, through Jesus Christ our Lord.
All	**Amen.**[2]

Hymn/Gloria

Use Peruvian[3] or other hymn type of Gloria. Whichever you use it should be sung with gusto – the first time for six weeks (unless used on Easter Eve).

Collect for the day or this prayer

NB: Please see note on the collect or prayer for the day in 'How to use this book' (p. 14).

Minister	Amazing God, by raising Jesus to life you have changed everything; make us people of hope and joy, for this is the start of a new life for us and all the world, through our Saviour Jesus Christ.
All	**Amen.**

WE LISTEN

Reading(s)

Easter Day is one of those occasions when it may be good to use all three readings.

Read the Old Testament reading from a scroll, and from somewhere unexpected, e.g. a balcony or other high point.

The Acts readings (must be used in a Church of England principal service); see 'Additional resource: Easter Sunday' at the end of this outline (p. 62) for an alternative version.

Even if you don't usually have a Gospel procession, this is the day to do so. Introduce the Gospel with ceremony and fanfare. If possible, proclaim the Gospel reading from memory or use a child who is a good, confident reader.

Talk

Begin by asking those who volunteered to tell us about something they have done for the first time to come forward and share the experience, giving it marks out of ten.

(If you have no prepared volunteers, then start here.)

Ask people if they can remember other exciting moments – give suggestions like the first time riding a bike without stabilizers, or the first time swimming in the sea, the first time in a plane, the first time speaking in public, etc. Say something similar to:

> There are sad first times and happy first times – there are special first times too. Sometimes it's because we didn't think something would ever happen, for example a person who walks out of hospital after a terrible accident (you may be able to find an example of such a scenario, e.g. a person celebrating the first birthday of a very premature child). Milestones like this are often celebrated and remembered in some way. It might be a party or it might be simply stored away in the memory bank of our minds.
>
> Imagine for a moment asking Mary what she did for the first time ever today: 'Well, I saw Jesus alive again!' How incredible was that? They knew Jesus had power over death – he had raised all sorts of people through his prayers, but no one ever expected that Jesus himself would return. Amazing! No wonder there were angels and earthquakes happening.
>
> Angels were there as heralds of a new birth. We usually think about angels at Christmas, when they were there to tell us the good news that Jesus had been born. Now they are telling us the good news that Jesus is alive again.

Talk about why the earthquake might have happened – it is a sign that what has happened will not just affect people but the whole of creation.

Invite two volunteers to the front.

Give one of them a large carrier or bin bag full of rubbish. Have a look in it and discuss contents – include food rubbish, a used tea towel, some sticking plasters, and broken things. These things remind us of the mess we make of our lives and our world – we are greedy, we don't help people, we break things, we hurt people.

Give the second volunteer a similar bag, but inside it have loads of confetti hearts.

> When Jesus came back to life it was wonderful. It was the best day ever because it was the day when God took all that was bad in the world (tell volunteer to hide bag behind them) and instead held out his hand (tell second volunteer to start walking towards people and then begin to shake the bag out over them) with so much love for the world, inviting everyone to make a new beginning.
>
> What have you done for the first time today? Discovered that Jesus is alive, and that God is love! Alleluia!

 ## WE RESPOND

Creed or statement of faith

There is a special Easter statement of faith, or you might keep with the familiarity of other all-age services and use something people know.

Making connections

Minister	We are celebrating the good news that Jesus lives – let's declare our faith in the resurrection of Jesus:
All	**Christ died for our sins in accordance with the Scriptures; he was buried; he was raised to life on the third day in accordance with the Scriptures; afterwards he appeared to his followers, and to all the apostles: this we have received, and this we believe. Amen.**[4]

Prayers

This prayer activity will work where there is enough space and where people are ready to move around for prayers.

Create five 'stations' or places of prayer, one of which should be the Easter garden in your church. At each station place the items indicated. Print out the suggested prayer themes below for each place.

Invite people to walk around, visit each station, and spend a moment praying there, doing the action as a sign of their prayer. As they do this, play music appropriate for Easter.

Butterflies – hope

If possible, place some fabric butterflies on a table alongside a picture of a chrysalis.

> Butterflies are a great sign of new life, freedom and hope.
>
> Pick up and hold a butterfly and think of a situation that needs to find the hope of Jesus' new life. Place it back down carefully as you say 'Amen' to your silent prayer.

Chrysalis – memories

If possible, place some large stones next to a picture of a chrysalis.

Place some sticky notes or paper as well.

> As you look at the chrysalis which looks so lifeless, think about situations in your life or the world that seem hard and difficult. Pick up a piece of paper and place it under or on the stones as a sign of your prayer.

Eggs – promise

Place a bowl of eggs and a bowl of mini-eggs next to each other – enough mini-eggs for everyone! (Provide an alternative for those who can't eat chocolate.)

> Eggs are great things! Sometimes they contain the promise of new life, sometimes they are simply a good, basic food. As you look at the eggs, give thanks to God for his promises for us and for the world. Take a mini-egg and, as you eat it, pray for peace and justice throughout the world.

Daffodils – joy

Place a large bunch of daffodils in a bright vase, together with a large empty plate and some sticky notes/paper slips.

> It's hard to look at daffodils and feel sad! The bright colour makes us feel joyful. As you look at them, give thanks to God for all that brings you joy today. Pick up a paper slip and place it on the plate as a sign of your thanks.

Easter garden – good news

Take a moment to stand/sit/kneel by the Easter garden. Pray that the good news that Jesus is alive will be real in your life today. As you leave, simply touch the rolled-away stone as a sign of your belief and trust in Jesus.

When everyone has returned to their seats, gather the prayers together in these or similar words:

Minister   Loving God, we thank you for the good news that Jesus is alive. Help us to live as people of joy and hope and to share that joy with all whom we meet. Amen.

OR

If the prayer stations won't work for your building or congregation, adapt the prayers either imaginatively, that is by inviting people to imagine in their minds each of the objects and pray accordingly, or use actions as below with these or similar words:

Butterflies

Invite people to make a butterfly shape by linking thumbs together and fluttering hands.

Minister   Amazing God, Risen Jesus, you bring hope and beauty into every situation. We pray for . . . and all places in our world that need to know your hope today.

Chrysalis

Invite people to fold their hands tightly into a ball shape.

Minister   Amazing God, Risen Jesus, you have shown that nothing is impossible to you. We pray today for those who feel they are living in difficult situations that are not easy to fix, and we ask that they may know that you are still with them.

Eggs

Invite people to join thumb tips and index-finger tips to make an oval shape, folding remaining fingers out of the way.

Minister   Amazing God, Risen Jesus, you have shown that you are faithful and keep your promise. We pray today for all those who are celebrating new beginnings in their families or in the community, and thank you for all those who bring us joy.

Daffodils

Invite people to place heels of palms together and cup hands with fingers loose like petals.

Minister   Amazing God, Risen Jesus, you have shown that you are worthy of our praise. We pray today for Christians everywhere that our hearts may be full of joy as we share the good news of Easter.

Easter garden

Invite everyone to turn towards the garden.

Voice   Amazing God, Risen Jesus, you come to each
one of us in the stillness of our hearts. We pray
in silence for ourselves as we commit ourselves
again to be your followers on this day and always.

If the service is a service of the word, it may be
appropriate to end the prayers with the Lord's
Prayer, before sharing the peace together.

If the service is a Eucharist, continue with the peace
followed by the offertory and the eucharistic prayer.
Involve different generations as appropriate.

The peace

Introduce the peace, using words that are familiar or
the special Easter greeting. It may be appropriate to
invite children to be with you and join in sharing
the peace.

Minister   The risen Christ came and stood among
his disciples and said, 'Peace be with you.'
Then were they glad when they saw the Lord.
Alleluia.[5]

An informal alternative to shaking hands is to have
one person standing in the middle with a bowl of
sweets (or wrapped mini-eggs) and encourage
people to take a chocolate and then give it to
someone else as they share the peace.

The offertory

Invite a family or children and young people to bring
forward the bread and wine, and involve children in
setting the table.

These can also be the ones to say:

Voice   With this bread that we bring

All   **we shall remember Jesus.**

Voice   With this wine that we bring

All   **we shall remember Jesus.**

Voice   Bread for his body, wine for his blood,
gifts from God to his table we bring.

All   **We shall remember Jesus.[6]**

The eucharistic prayer

Suggestion: use Prayer D with a child introducing
the refrain; or use one of the new eucharistic prayers
for use with children present.

(NB: If using the extended preface for Easter[7] please
remember to include the word 'children' in line 10:
through his death and resurrection Jesus restored the
image of his glory in everyone, not just adults!)

Follow with the breaking of the bread and the
invitation to communion.

Distribution

Invite people to write or draw a prayer on an angel
shape and then place the angels around the font.

 # WE GO OUT

Notices may be included at this point as part of
moving the focus to our Christian lives.

Blessing

Minister   May Christ,
who out of defeat brings new hope and a new
future,
fill you with his new life;
and the blessing . . .[8]

Voice   Jesus is alive!

Voices   We have heard the good news (*use the choir or
other group*).

All   **Let's share it with the world!**

Voice   Jesus is alive!

Voices   We have heard the good news.

All   **Let's live it in our lives. Alleluia!**

Minister   Go in the peace of Christ. Alleluia. Alleluia!

All   **Thanks be to God. Alleluia. Alleluia!**

Notes

1 *Common Worship: Services and Prayers for the Church of England*, London: Church House Publishing, 2000, p. 167.
2 *New Patterns for Worship*, London: Church House Publishing, 2008, p. 96, B78.
3 *Complete Anglican Hymns Old and New*, Stowmarket: Kevin Mayhew, 1976, 966.
4 *New Patterns for Worship*, p. 165, E10.
5 *New Patterns for Worship*, p. 274, H22.
6 *Common Worship: Services and Prayers*, p. 292.
7 *Common Worship: Services and Prayers*, p. 317.
8 *New Patterns for Worship*, p. 308, J85.

Eyewitness

A version of Acts 10.34–43

You will need two people, a handbell to ring.

Voice   (*ringing a bell like a town crier*) Roll up, roll up! Hear the latest news!

(*Peter steps forward.*)

Peter   I'm Peter and have I got news for you!!

You've already heard about the message God sent through Jesus. It was a message of peace for everyone who listened and acted. That message spread from Jerusalem, to Galilee, to all Judea.

It all began with John the Baptist, then Jesus himself went around healing people, telling stories and changing lives. I know, I was there. I saw it for myself – and not just the good bits. I was right there when they put him to death on the cross.

But I was also there when the story went on. Because three days after he died God raised Jesus from the dead: and we saw him for ourselves. Then he told us, me, Peter, and others of his friends, to go and tell the good news to all the world.

And this is the news for you – Jesus is not dead, but alive!

And there's more. Everyone who believes in him will find forgiveness of sins through his name!

It's amazing. You'd better believe it!

Voice   (*town-crier style*) Hear the word of the Lord from the book of Acts!

Fire, wind and adventure

Pentecost is a much less well-known festival, both in our culture and even in the church calendar, yet it is not just theologically significant but also rich in some of our more well-known symbols. The energy and excitement that emanate from the story in Acts should be infectious, and the readings clearly affirm that this is something for everyone of every age and stage of life. There is also a sense in which Pentecost acts as the culmination of the great Easter mystery and also the beginning of a great adventure: the life of the Church. It is this theme of adventure that is picked up in the outline for worship. This worship is one that would work very well outside; for the very adventurous that might even include holding the Eucharist outside, whereas for others it might mean holding part of the service outdoors, then moving inside, or at least moving between the two.

Key lectionary readings

NB: Please see note on lectionary readings in 'How to use this book' (p. 13).

Pentecost requires the set lectionary readings for the day in a Church of England principal service.

Ezekiel 37.1–14 'Breathe life'
Acts 2.1–21 'Talking fire'
John 15.26, 27; 16.4b–15 'Receive'

Preparation

Set up several poles outside the church decorated with red and white streamers; decorate inside with similar streamers. Tie red and white balloons appropriately. Create very large flame shapes from yellow, orange, red fabric or crepe paper and place over the doors to the church.

You will need

- Poles
- Red and white streamers
- Red and white balloons
- Fabric or paper in yellow, orange and red
- Mini hot-air balloon (optional)

 ## WE GATHER

Either gather outside or use the opening hymn to process outside. Provide chairs for those unable to stand for any length of time. If you are not going to go outside, simply follow the pattern below.

Opening hymn

Formal Introduction

Minister	Alleluia! Christ is risen!
All	**He is risen indeed! Alleluia!**
	(*The following could be accompanied by an emphatic drum rhythm. Repeat three or four times, encouraging congregation to join in with last line and others as they feel able.*)
Voice	The wind of God is blowing! The fire of God is blazing! The joy of God is flowing in this place!
Minister	This is the day when the Church celebrates the coming of the Holy Spirit. It's a day of celebration and a day of adventure. It's a day of praise and a day of prayer. Let's imagine we are gathered with the followers of Jesus as they wait and pray, day after day.
	(*Silence for 30 seconds.*)

Voice   They were all together in one place, praying and waiting, praying and waiting, praying and waiting.

        (*Silence for 30 seconds followed either by prayer of preparation OR:*)

Voice   Almighty God,
help us today to be open to your Spirit,
to hear your word, proclaim your glory,
and celebrate the good news of Jesus Christ.
Amen.

We say sorry

Making connections

Minister   Sometimes we forget about God's Holy Spirit at work in our world. Sometimes we forget to listen to God or to one another. Sometimes we are too lazy to understand and care for our world. In the stillness we come before God and ask his forgiveness.

        (*Invite people to turn slowly in circle, looking round the world.*)

Voice   Lord, we admit we neglect your creation and ignore the needs of the world.
Fill us with your Spirit.
Lord, have mercy.

All   **Lord, have mercy.**

        (*Invite people to stand very still as if rooted to the spot.*)

Voice   Lord, we admit that we do nothing when we should take action.
Fill us with your Spirit.
Christ, have mercy.

All   **Christ, have mercy.**

        (*Invite people to close their eyes and become aware of what they can hear.*)

Voice   Lord, we admit we forget to listen for your word.
Fill us with your Spirit.
Lord, have mercy.

All   **Lord, have mercy.**

Minister   May the Father of all mercies
cleanse *us* from *our* sins,
and restore *us* in his image
to the praise and glory of his name,
through Jesus Christ our Lord.

All   **Amen.**[1]

Hymn/Gloria

Use Peruvian[2] or other hymn type of Gloria.

Collect for the day or this prayer

NB: Please see note on the collect or prayer for the day in 'How to use this book' (p. 14).

Minister   Holy Spirit of God,
set our hearts on fire with love,
give us courage and faith
to be your people, build your Church
and change your world,
through Jesus Christ our Lord.

All   **Amen.**

 WE LISTEN

Reading(s)

Ezekiel

There are several creative versions of this reading, e.g. www.emergingchurch.org, *The Big Bible Story Book* (see p. 98), or you could play 'Dem bones' as a piece of music!

Acts

See drama in 'Additional resource: Pentecost' at the end of this outline (pp. 67–8).

Gospel

At the end, repeat the words: 'This is the Gospel of the Lord', getting louder and louder. If outside, turn to different directions while doing so.

Talk

NB: This talk involves going outside and inside the church. For congregations where this is not appropriate, there is a variation below.

Ask who has ever had an adventure. Say something similar to:

Adventures are the themes of lots of books and stories.

Ask for any ideas. Then tell people about the Pixar film, *Up*.

This film is all about adventure. It begins with the main character, Carl, as a small boy who longs for adventures. As an old man, widowed, he wants to create the adventure his dead wife never had. He ties balloons all over his house until one day it floats off. A small boy, Russell, is accidentally taken along for the ride.

This adventure begins with balloons.

Talk about hot-air balloons and how they work, for example that there is a flame of fire which heats the air and lifts the balloon. (You can buy mini hot-air balloons; if you want to use one, test it out first to see if it works.)

> God's spirit came at Pentecost with wind and fire . . . and then all the followers of Jesus were off on an amazing adventure.

Ask who is ready to go on an adventure.

Set off and walk to the gate or outside entrance (or simply walk out on to the pavement) of the church. When you arrive, talk about how the adventure made all the followers of Jesus go out onto the streets and begin telling people about Jesus. Some of them would go much further, travelling all over the known world, spreading the news.

Then walk to an entrance into the church (this might be the only door or, if you have more than one entrance, choose a less-used door, which should be open). Stop and talk about how the adventure also involved their learning how to be God's people together, worshipping, praying and sharing.

Then, if possible, walk through the church and back outside again.

Talk about how the Holy Spirit is still at work, encouraging us to go out into the world.

> Some people will have adventures for Jesus that take them all over the world. God still needs people willing to go to other countries or to different kinds of people.
>
> Remind people of the film *Up* – Carl went far away for an adventure, but then discovered the diary that his wife had written. She had written that the greatest adventure was being with him, her husband. Gods also wants us to be on the adventure of learning to be God's people in this place and in places where we work, learn and play.
>
> Wherever we are, whatever we do, God's Holy Spirit is with us, giving us the power to do what needs to be done.

Additional notes if the talk is taking place entirely inside

The talk can be done inside but, instead of everyone moving around, simply send groups of active volunteers to the different places.

Attach a Scripture to the gates (or outer space), e.g. 'Go into all the world and make disciples.' Attach a Scripture to the door, e.g. 'Now the whole group of those who believed were of one heart and mind.' The group going out can bring these back. While they are gone, invite the congregation to talk together about the work of God's Spirit in the world today.

 ## WE RESPOND

Creed or statement of faith

Making connections

Minister	God's Spirit is building us into God's people. Let's declare together the things we believe:
All	**We believe in God the Father** [and mother], **from whom every family in heaven and on earth is named.**
	We believe in God the Son, who lives in our hearts through faith, and fills us with his love.
	We believe in God the Holy Spirit, who strengthens us with power from on high.
	We believe in one God; Father, Son and Holy Spirit. Amen.[3]

Prayers

Choose the prayer activity depending on how much movement you have already been able to introduce into the service. If the whole service has been indoors, you may wish to go outside for the prayers, or if the service has been outside, perhaps simply sitting for these actions (inside or out) may be more appropriate. Use these or similar words:

Voice Breathe on us, God, with your Spirit (*invite people to blow gently*).
Loving God, we pray for the life of the Church and for ourselves. Help us to be open to the work of your Spirit, taking us on an adventure as God's people. Be with all those who are leaders and give them boldness to lead people out. Help us in our own lives to have the

courage to go where you are calling us to go,
and to know that you are always with us.
Lord, hear our prayer

All   **please.**

Voice   Challenge us, God, with your Spirit (*invite people
to make flame movements with hands*).
Loving God, we pray for our world, and ask
that your Spirit give strength to those who
speak out for justice and work for peace.
We pray especially for (*insert current situations
here*) and ask that you give men, women and
children hope for the future.
Lord, hear our prayer

All   **please.**

Voice   Teach us, God, by your Spirit (*invite people to
put hands to ears*).
Loving God, we pray for the live of our families
and our community. Help us to listen well to
each other and to learn more about love in
our lives. Give wisdom to all who teach and
encourage others, especially remembering those
who work in this place, in our places of learning
and places of help.
Lord, hear our prayer

All   **please.**

Voice   Heal us, God, by your Spirit (*invite people to
place hands on heart*).
Loving God, we pray for all those we know
who need your healing and for those known
only to you. Give strength to those who are
struggling with physical pain and be close to
those who are sad or alone. Help each of us to
hear your Spirit and reach out in help to those
around us.
Lord, hear our prayer

All   **please.**

Voice   Encourage us, God, by your Spirit (*invite people
to cup hands around mouths*).
Loving God, we pray for ourselves, that you give
us the confidence we need to share the good
news of your love with those around us. Fill us
with your Spirit today, so that we may grow
more and more in the knowledge of your love.
Lord, hear our prayer

All   **please.**

End prayers in usual way for Eucharist or, if a non-
eucharistic service, then end with the Lord's Prayer.

The peace

The minister introduces the peace, using these or
similar words. It may be appropriate to invite
children to be with you and join in sharing the peace.

Minister   God has made us one in Christ.
He has set his seal upon us, and as a pledge of
what is to come,
has given the Spirit to dwell in our hearts.
Alleluia.
The peace of the Lord be always with you

All   **and also with you.**[4]

If the service is a Eucharist, continue in the usual way.

 WE GO OUT

Notices may be included at this point as part of
moving the focus to our Christian lives.

Blessing

Minister   May God's Holy Spirit be in your life (*place
hand on heart*).
May God's Holy Spirit be in our world (*sweep
hand out in front*).
May God's Holy Spirit be love between us
(*hold hands*).
And the blessing of God,
Father, Son and Holy Spirit,
be with us, this day and always.

All   **Amen.**

Dismissal

Minister   We go into the world, filled with the Spirit
to walk in God's light, to rejoice in God's love
and to reflect God's glory.[5]
Go in the peace of Christ. Alleluia. Alleluia!

All   **Thanks be to God. Alleluia. Alleluia!**[6]

Give away balloons as people leave.

Notes

1 *New Patterns for Worship*, London: Church House Publishing, 2008, p. 96, B78.
2 *Complete Anglican Hymns Old and New*, Stowmarket: Kevin Mayhew, 1976, 966.
3 *New Patterns for Worship*, p. 166, E12.
4 *New Patterns for Worship*, p. 275, H27.
5 *New Patterns for Worship*, p. 315, J116 (adapted), copyright © Trustees for Methodist Church Purposes. Used by permission of
Methodist Publishing.
6 *Common Worship: Services and Prayers for the Church of England*, London: Church House Publishing, 2000, p. 227.

Reading for two voices and a chorus based on Acts 2.1–21

This needs careful rehearsing. It works well if the choir or similar group act as the chorus.

Chorus (*getting louder*) Listen, listen, listen, listen, listen, listen!

Voice 1 It was the day of Pentecost

Voice 2 and all the followers of Jesus were in one place.

Voice 1 Suddenly . . .

Voice 2 Suddenly . . . there was the sound of a rushing wind

Chorus (*getting louder*) Woosh, woosh, woosh, woosh, woosh, woosh!

Voice 1 a violent rushing wind from heaven

Chorus (*even louder*) Whoosh, whoosh, whoosh, whoosh!

Voice 2 (*shouting*) and flames of fire appeared on everyone's head

Chorus Pshwwh, pshwwh, pshwwh!

Voices 1 and 2 together and everyone began to talk in other languages

Chorus Mutter, mutter, mutter, mutter!

Voice 1 and everyone

Voice 2 could understand everyone else.

Chorus Bonjour!!

(*Pause.*)

Voice 1 There were lots of visitors in Jerusalem from all over the known world.

Voice 2 They were amazed at what was happening and rushed up to find out more.

Chorus (*chanted in a monotone*) There were Parthians, Medes, Elamites and Mesopotamians, there were Judeans and Cappadocians, people from Pontus and Asia, Phrygia, Pamphylia, Egypt, Libya, Rome, Crete and Arabia . . .

But none from England!

Voice 1 And everyone could hear their own language being spoken!

Voice 2 It was very confusing

Voice 1 so some said they must be drunk.

(*Pause.*)

Voice 1 Peter stepped forward to speak to the crowd.

Voice 2 'It's only nine in the morning!' he said. 'We're not drunk!'

Voice 1 No – all this is happening just as the prophet Joel said.

Voice 2 He said there will come a day when there will be

Chorus visions and prophecy

Voice 1 not just for a few

Chorus but for men and women, sons and daughters, boys and girls

Voice 2 even slaves!

Chorus Even slaves!

Voice 1 And there will be signs of fire and mist and darkness and noise

Voice 2 for it is the great and glorious day of the Lord.

Chorus (*loudly*) And everyone who calls on the name of the Lord . . . shall be saved!

Festivals Together (London: SPCK). Copyright © Sandra Millar 2012

Father's Day

Holding the baby

Unlike Mothering Sunday, Father's Day holds no place in the church calendar. Yet over the past fifty years it has grown massively in importance within UK culture. Children will prepare for it with the same enthusiasm as they employ for their mums. The Church is sometimes reluctant to engage with, yet alone enjoy, these kinds of cultural events, taking a cynical or even a slightly superior attitude towards an occasion invented by the card industry. Yet there is also an increasing awareness in the Church of the need to communicate with men, and part of that is to affirm fathering. This service uses readings specially chosen for the day and offers ideas that allow us to give thanks for the fathering we have known in our lives, remember the disappointments, pray for families, and encounter in unexpected ways the God who is Father of all. This outline could be used on a Sunday in church or in another location at another point during the week – the school hall after Saturday football practice, for example.

Key readings

Deuteronomy 32.6b–14 'God lets us soar'
John 15.9–11 (12–17) 'Love and fruitfulness'

Preparation

You will need

- A large piece of paper or old bed sheet and marker/fabric pens
- An indoor goal net or basket-ball hoop
- A container with lots of small balls, e.g. table-tennis size, and an empty bucket
- OR a dartboard

- A selection of men's birthday and other cards, showing stereotypical 'men's' activities
- A photo of a dad throwing and catching baby, e.g. from a birthday card or by searching Internet images
- A card or screen with the word 'Trust'
- A selection of items (or pictures of them), e.g. a football, laptop, hammer, carrier bag, baby sling
- A computer ready for use; a projector lined up and ready for screen or suitable wall
- Mini 'credit cards' with a picture of a father and child on one side and a short Scripture on the back, e.g. 'Let the beloved of the LORD rest secure in him, for God shields them all day long, and the one the LORD loves rests between his shoulders' (Deuteronomy 33.12, NIV, adapted). (These can be made using a desktop publishing programme or by hand.)
- Single red roses to give away
- A copy of the Luther Vandross song, 'Dance with my father again' or Eric Clapton, 'In my father's eyes', or Professor Green, 'At your inconvenience' (a bit radical!), and the means to play it

Before the service

You will need to put up a large sheet of paper or old sheet divided into four sections with the heading: 'Things about Dads'. The sections are headed: glad, sad, special, funny.

As people (of all ages) arrive, invite them to go over to the sheet and write things into the different sections. Delay the start of the service to allow everyone to have a go!

If you want you could put a short explanation nearby, e.g.

Please write as many things as you like. You could also write about a granddad or step-dad . . . or memories from long ago.

- *Glad* – things you are thankful for, e.g. My dad makes great burgers!
- *Sad* – things that are difficult, e.g. I still miss my dad after twenty years.
- *Special* – things that are unique, e.g. My dad can stand on his head.
- *Funny* – things that make you laugh, e.g. When Dad plays air guitar.

 ## WE GATHER

Opening hymn

Informal welcome

Making ready

Invite different people to say each sentence from different parts of the church.

Voice 1	Thank you, God, for our dads.
Voice 2	Thank you, God, for our mums.
Voice 3	Thank you, God, for our families.
Voice 4	Thank you, God, for the family of the Church.
Voice 5	Thank you, God, that you are our God and Father.

(Invite everyone to join in a 'Mexican wave' praise shout moving up and down the church. Each row is invited in turn to jump up, wave arms high and shout: 'Thank you, God!' To make this effective it is best to have one or two leaders who are enthusiastically running up and down the aisle, reminding each row when it is their turn to stand, raise their arms and shout.)

All   **Thank you, God!**

We say sorry

Making connections

Minister   In all our services we take time to think about things that have gone wrong, even on a happy day like this. Fathers get it wrong, children get it wrong, everyone gets it wrong. Sometimes it's our fault, sometimes it's just that there are bad and sad things in our world. Sin is an old word meaning to 'miss the mark', so this morning, after the words, we are going to say sorry or

feel sad by coming forward and picking up a ball and placing it in the bucket in front of the net, just as if we had missed the goal. While we do this some music will play.

Voice   We are sad because we have hurt other people. Lord, have mercy.

All   **Lord, have mercy.**

Voice   We are sad because we have been hurt by others. Christ, have mercy.

All   **Christ, have mercy.**

Voice   We are sad for all the hurts in God's world. Lord, have mercy.

All   **Lord, have mercy.**

(Listen to some music, e.g. Luther Vandross, 'Dance with my father again', or Eric Clapton, 'In my father's eyes', or Professor Green, 'At your inconvenience', as people move forward to place the balls in front of the net.

When everyone has returned to their seats:)

Minister   May the God of love and power
forgive *us* and free *us* from *our* sins,
heal and strengthen *us* by his Spirit,
and raise *us* to new life in Christ our Lord.

All   **Amen.**[1]

Gloria/hymn or song

Collect for the day or this prayer

NB: Please see note on the collect or prayer for the day in 'How to use this book' (p. 14).

Minister   Heavenly Father,
you sent your Son Jesus
to show us your love and lead us into freedom,
help us to share that love
with our families and our friends,
and to learn from you
how to bring life to the world.

All   **Amen.**

 ## WE LISTEN

Reading(s)

Suggestion: if using only one reading, choose Deuteronomy.

Deuteronomy: see *The Message* for a different version.

John: read verses (*Contemporary English Version* Bible).

There are also some moving poems and readings about being a father, e.g. 'First lesson' by Phyllis McGinley[2]; 'Starlight' by Philip Levine[3] or, if you have the technology, you might like to go to Michael Rosen's website and show one of his poems, e.g. 'Don't tell your mother' or 'I'm tired' (they are all funny!). He also has some moving poems about the loss of his son.

Talk

Invite some people either to bring the 'banner' to the front or to read things from it. Talk about it with the congregation, add other memories. Say something similar to:

Dads are clearly pretty amazing!

Show lots of 'men's' birthday cards – with football, cars, fishing, drinking.

They are clearly an active bunch who take risks, do things, and have fun.

Show picture of baby being thrown and caught. Dads are usually the ones who play these kinds of adventurous games, bringing laughter and joy.

An interesting observation of family life is this: the first parent to throw a baby into the air is almost always Dad. It is Dad who pushes the swing that little bit too high, Dad who encourages the climb to the top of the slide or to run that bit further into the sea. Mum is usually sitting by saying, 'Take care!' Fathers teach us about risk . . . and about trust.

Parenting is good news – it is a delight and a joy, bringing us times of play and laughter. But there is another side of the coin: many people feel abandoned and lost by those who should parent them. Jesus reaches out to them to show the love of the Father, for fathering is also about compassion and care, providing and loving, as well as fun and laughter . . . and underpinning all these things is the big T word: Trust.

(You could put this word on a card or screen.)

The reading from Deuteronomy tells us the same kinds of thing. It's a wonderful word picture of God enjoying his people, soaring with them on high, feeding them the best things, exploring the world. It's a joyful and fun image of relationship. Jesus talked about the same relationship with God the Father, a relationship that will be full of delight – and, yes, fun!

Invite a parent and child to come to the front and demonstrate the trust game (where the child has her back to the father and then falls backwards, knowing the father will catch her). That's the real heart of the relationship. Or, if you can't get a volunteer to do this, then simply get a dad to walk about with a smaller child (under three) high on his shoulders.

God is a Father – and sometimes the sort of picture we have of God the Father is that of a safe old man, who is cuddly and, well, a bit tame. God is a cuddly Dad when we need a cuddly Dad – especially for those times when we are sad, or when our own parents have not been there for us or have even hurt us. But God is also a God of adventure who wants to bring his people into life.

We love dads because they are fun. We love them because they provide for us. We love them because they can fix things when they are broken. But most of all we love them because they love us . . . and it's the love that allows us to trust them for all the other things.

The love of our families – dads, mums, brothers, sister, grandparents and others – all of it helps us to understand God's great love. Today we especially give thanks for fathers and remember that God is our Father – we can trust him, love him – and play!

 # WE RESPOND

Creed or statement of faith

Making connections

Minister We've been thinking about love and about families, so let's stand and speak out together what we believe:

All **We believe in God the Father,
from whom every family
in heaven and on earth is named.**

**We believe in God the Son,
who lives in our hearts through faith,
and fills us with his love.**

**We believe in God the Holy Spirit,
who strengthens us
with power from on high.**

**We believe in one God;
Father, Son and Holy Spirit.
Amen.**[4]

Prayers

Either invite people to hold out the items or pictures or show them on a screen. You could also invite a dad to type the words of the prayers 'live' onto the pictures. Use different generations of fathers, mothers and children to hold items and to pray, using one or more voices, adapting as appropriate to your situation.

Hold out football or similar item, or show picture.

Voice   God our Father, thank you for all the fun things in our lives, for freedom to play and moments of laughter. We remember today those whose lives are sad because they are alone or afraid or unable to be with those they love. Help them to know that you are their Father.
Lord, in your mercy . . . hear our prayer.

(Hold out laptop or similar item, or show picture.)

Voice   God our Father, thank you for the work that goes on in our world, in offices and factories, in shops and schools, in fields and hospitals. We pray that as our dads and others go about their work they will know your presence and that you will help them to work with wisdom and honesty.
Lord in your mercy . . . hear our prayer.

(Hold out shopping bag or similar item, or show picture.)

Voice   God our Father, thank you for our homes and families and for our food. We remember those in the world who are struggling because of war and injustice, especially children who have no one to provide for them. Help us to share what we have with them and give courage to all who work for peace.
Lord, in your mercy . . . hear our prayer.

(Hold out baby sling or similar item, or show picture.)

Voice   God our Father, thank you for your love for each one of us. Help us in this church to show that love to one another and to the community around us so that everyone may come to know that you are a Father to all.
Lord, in your mercy . . . hear our prayer.

If this is a non-eucharistic service, use the Lord's Prayer to gather the prayers together. If it is a Eucharist, end prayers in the usual way.

The peace

Minister   God makes peace within us – let us claim it.
God makes peace between us – let us share it.
The peace of the Lord be with you

All   **and also with you.**[5]

72

Suggestion: if this is a Eucharist, use children and families to bring up bread and wine and to take offering where appropriate. When the table is ready, invite a father and children or a group of dads/granddads to say the offertory prayer using this form:

Voices   With this bread that we bring (*hold out bread*)
All   **we shall remember Jesus.**
With this wine that we bring (*hold out wine*)
All   **we shall remember Jesus.**

Bread for his body, wine for his blood, gifts from God to his table we bring.
All   **We shall remember Jesus.**[6]

Suggestion: Use Eucharistic Prayer D – using same group to say the 'This is our story' refrain.

(During the distribution of communion, invite children and others to continue writing things on the large sheet/paper.)

 **WE GO OUT**

If you are using roses to give away, invite some children to bring them to the front and pray:

Minister   Lord our God, thank you for the gift of fathers,
for all they show us of your love,
for all the joy they bring us,
for all the laughter we share.

Be with them in times of play and times of rest,
in times of delight and times of despair,
in the beauty and in the sadness,
in their work and in their homes
on this and every day. Amen.

Blessing

Minister   May the God who is Father to all the world be close to you.
May the Son who showed us the way to God lead you.
May the Spirit who brings us together in love enfold you
and the blessing of God, Father, Son and Spirit, be with you and those you love,
this day and always.
All   **Amen.**

The dismissal

Voice   We go in joy and laughter.
All   **We go!**
Voice   We go to play and to share.

All	**We go!**	
Voice	We go to learn and to love.	
All	**We go!**	
Voice	We go in the name of God, Father, Son and Spirit.	
All	**We go!**	
Minister	Go in peace to love and serve the Lord.	
All	**In the name of Christ. Amen.**	

As people leave the church give either a single rose or a small 'credit card' with a picture of a father and child on one side and a short Scripture on the back, e.g. 'Let the beloved of the Lord rest secure in him, for God shields them all day long, and the one the Lord loves rests between his shoulders' (Deuteronomy 33.12, NIV).

Notes

1 *New Patterns for Worship*, London: Church House Publishing, 2008, p. 97, B80.
2 From Michele Guinness (ed.), *Tapestry of Voices: Meditations in Celebration of Women*, London: Triangle, 1993.
3 From Neil Astley (ed.), *Being Alive*, Tarset: Bloodaxe, 2004.
4 *New Patterns for Worship*, p. 166, E12.
5 The St Hilda Community, *New Women Included: A Book of Services and Prayers*, London: SPCK, 1996, p. 55.
6 *Common Worship: Services and Prayers for the Church of England*, London: Church House Publishing, 2000, p. 292.

Harvest

Too much, too bad

Harvest is unusual among the various festivals of the church and community year, in that it is elective – that means you get to choose when to hold the event. A church can choose the date, the time, the place and the content. There are no fixed readings, although there are many suggestions. Harvest Festival is a relatively recent addition to the church calendar, taking us back to those halcyon Victorian rural dreams, when the local vicar or parson was a linchpin in the community and the local church and community would be drawn together to celebrate all that God had provided. There was also a clever mixing of ancient folk customs around the celebration of a harvest successfully completed with a sense of praise and thanksgiving to the Creator.

More recently Harvest Festival services have been reworked to resonate more effectively with contemporary concerns. Almost every aid agency with Christian roots, and some without, offers resources for Harvest, and churches of every type have developed themes around environmental issues. They have also been reworked with a view to engaging those on the fringes of church, with involvement of schools and other community groups. In some rural communities, Harvest remains the service with the highest attendance – just outdoing Christmas and certainly overtaking Easter (this may be due to the F-factor: the food that is provided afterwards!).

This service outline can be used in church, school or other location and focuses on thanksgiving and generosity as traditional Harvest themes. It also assumes that there will be a traditional harvest offering of goods. The key reading is not a traditional harvest reading, but gives an opportunity to do something different.

Key readings

Psalm 65.5–13 'It's a wonderful world'
Luke 19.1–9 'From grabbing to giving'

Preparation

You will need

- Six boxes – ideally matching wooden crates, but any box that will stand by itself and has one side open will work. These boxes will need to be built into a display in an accessible part of the worship space. They contain: a world map; a loaf; a first-aid kit; a dancing shoe; a stole and a Bible; and a small mirror

- A big collection of autumn leaves

- Boxes or bags for the produce brought in by the congregation (according to local custom)

- At least four prepared drama volunteers

- A selection of gift boxes or wrapped boxes

- Four pairs of over-sized sunglasses

- The words 'sharing', 'giving' and 'thanking' written large enough for everyone to see on cards/overhead projector

- Enough gift tags for everyone

 ## WE GATHER

Minister	The Lord be with you
All	**And also with you.**

Informal welcome

Introduction and presentation of gifts

Invite people to hold up the harvest gifts they have brought with them.

Invite them to look up to the roof – and beyond to the sky.

Voice   Thank you, God, for your goodness that blesses us and the earth.
You are generous.

All   **Thank you, God.**

(Invite people to look around at the congregation and beyond the walls.)

Voice   Thank you, God, for the people who made this food and those who will share in it.
You are generous.

All   **Thank you, God.**

(Invite people to look down at the ground and the earth beneath.)

Voice   Thank you, God, for this place, this (village/town/city), this church and for your faithful love over many generations.
You are generous.

All   **Thank you, God.**

Opening hymn with offering of harvest gifts

You might like to have boxes ready and place the gifts straight into them. Arrange some items in a display as well.

Making connections

Minister   Harvest makes us aware of how much we have to enjoy, but it also makes us aware of how often we fail to take care of the world and those around us. It's also autumn, a time when the leaves fall, reminding us that sometimes we need to let go of things so that new things can happen. As we scatter leaves this morning, so we remember all the wrong choices we have made, the things we have not bothered to do, and the things we did on purpose that have hurt other people, hurt ourselves and hurt God.

Invite people to come forward and collect a handful of leaves and scatter them in front of the altar. While this is happening, play appropriate music. (If you are working with a school, they could prepare a song to sing at this point.)

When everyone has returned to their seats, arrange for some young people to sweep up and remove the leaves, then pray in these or similar words:

Voice   Lord God, we are selfish, we are greedy, we are wasteful of all that you have given us.
Sometimes we forget to say thank you.
Lord, have mercy.

All   **Lord, have mercy.**

Voice   Sometimes we ignore the needs of others.
Christ, have mercy.

All   **Christ, have mercy.**

Voice   Sometimes we just can't be bothered to live your way.
Lord, have mercy.

All   **Lord, have mercy.**

Voice   But we are sorry and ask that you forgive us.

Minister   May the Father of all mercies
cleanse *us* from *our* sins,
and restore *us* in his image
to the praise and glory of his name,
through Jesus Christ our Lord.

All   **Amen.**[1]

Collect for the day or this prayer

See note on the collect or prayer for the day in 'How to use this book' (p. 14).

Minister   Creator God, you make all things
and give us the earth and the seasons,
the rain, the sun and the wind;
make us thankful people with generous hearts,
ready to share your goodness and love
with all creation;
through Jesus Christ our Lord . . .

All   **Amen.**

 WE LISTEN

(You may also need or want to include presentations from school at this point.)

Read Psalm 65.5–13 from *The Message*.

Read Luke in usual way (as the talk is a dramatic retelling of story).

Talk

You will need one or two adults/teens at the side with the gift-wrapped boxes ready. Say something similar to:

> Zacchaeus? People are wondering what on earth this has to do with harvest. Do we have to give thanks for trees to climb?

Volunteer who is Zac stands at front with open arms.

> Now Zac was a man who liked things. As he began to earn money, so he began to acquire some things.

Someone comes forward with a box. Zac takes it, and puts it behind him. Repeat a couple of times.

> Zac liked his things. He liked to look at them and admire them. He wanted more. And more. So he cheated a bit here and there to get more things.

Someone comes and puts a box in Zac's arms. This time he holds it. The person adds another box.

> He stored up more and more things (pile boxes on in rapid succession) until he had so much stuff he couldn't see where he was going. He couldn't see that other people had much less than him. He couldn't reach out to help – or to ask for help. He couldn't even move very far from his house! (Place sunglasses over his eyes.)
>
> Poor Zac, aah!
>
> But then Zac heard that Jesus was coming to town. He managed to find his way out of his house. But he couldn't get to the front of the crowd. No one would help him or give him a hand. Zac was a real Billy-no-mates. He had loads of stuff, but no friends. After all, he couldn't reach out to others himself. So he had to climb that tree . . . and then things began to happen.
>
> First, Jesus came to eat at his house! He came and shared Zac's – and Mrs Zac's – food. Zac learned about sharing. He put down his things and sat with Jesus.
>
> Then Zac realized he had more than enough stuff – and began to give it away (get volunteer Zac to give boxes around congregation, helped by others). He learned about giving.
>
> Suddenly he realized his hands were empty. He could see where he was going and reach out to touch other people. He was free! He learned

about thanking. Jesus turned and told everyone salvation – life, freedom, healing – had come that day! Hurray!

Invite three more volunteers to come forward.

> In our world and in our lives we might not collect things like Zac did. But . . .

Begin piling some of the harvest foods into the hands of a volunteer. Pile on quite a lot and then put sunglasses over eyes.

> We have so much food in our lives we no longer see that there are people who are going hungry.

Begin piling books, laptop, school stuff on a second person. Then put sunglasses on.

> We have so many opportunities to learn, we forget that there are people who can't even go to school.

Invite lots of other volunteers to crowd round a third person. Then put on sunglasses.

> Some of us have so many friends and people who love us that we no longer look out for those who are lonely and unloved.
>
> This has everything to do with Harvest.

Three key words (on cards/overhead projector, etc): sharing, giving, thanking.

> Sometimes our lives are so full of things – possessions, anxiety, being important, coming first – that we also find it hard to see where we are going, or to reach out to others. When we share in hospitality and friendship, when we give away generously to others, and when we are thankful for all that God has given us, then we are able to enjoy all of God's world together with all God's people.

 # WE RESPOND

Creed or statement of faith

Making connections

Minister We share together as God's family, remembering all that we believe:

Do you believe and trust in God the Father, source of all being and life, the one for whom we all exist?

All **We believe and trust in him.**

Minister	Do you believe and trust in God the Son, who took our human nature, died for us and rose again?
All	**We believe and trust in him.**
Minister	Do you believe and trust in God the Holy Spirit, who gives life to the people of God and makes Christ known in the world?
All	**We believe and trust in him.**
Minister	This is the faith of the Church.
All	**This is our faith.** **We believe and trust in one God,** **Father, Son and Holy Spirit.** **Amen.**[2]

Prayers

Place the six boxes at the front, each with one of the objects in.

If you have a congregation who are able to do this, split into groups of about six to twelve.

One person from each group comes forward and takes an object. (In a large congregation you will need to have more than one of each object available.)

Each group has one minute to pray for themes that emerge from that object, before returning it and choosing another.

At the end gather all the prayers in these or similar words:

Minister	Loving God, you shower us with good things and you know all the needs we have. You listen to our prayers and hear the unspoken words in our hearts. Hear our prayers today, in Jesus' name. Amen.

OR

Invite someone to show each object and introduce a theme as indicated. Then invite people to pray by themselves or with another person for a minute for the theme.

- Map of the world – for every place where there is war and injustice
- Loaf – for everyone who is struggling to find food or make ends meet
- First-aid kit – for all who are unwell and for those who care

- Dancing shoe – for all who help us show joy in our lives
- Stole and Bible – for the Church
- Mirror – for ourselves.

OR

Invite school or other group to prepare prayers using the objects as their starting point

OR

Offer formal prayers while someone takes an object from the box and walks around showing it to people:

Map of the world

Voice	Creator God, your world is wonderful, full of delight and difference. We pray today for all who care for the world and for those who work to bring us understanding. We pray for those places where life is demanding, for those living in hostile climates caused by nature or by human beings. In every place bring your hope and healing. Lord, hear our prayer
All	**please.**

Loaf

Voice	Generous God, we pray today for all who work to bring us food and for all who speak out for those who have little food. We pray for those who will not have enough to eat today, and for all those who are working to bring help. In every place bring your hope and healing. Lord, hear our prayer
All	**please.**

First-aid kit

Voice	Healing God, we pray today for all who endure pain in mind or body and for those who help. We pray for those working in hospitals and those in research, those who work in our community and those caring out of love. In every place bring your hope and healing. Lord, hear our prayer
All	**please.**

Dancing shoe

Voice	Joyful God, we pray today for all who bring us delight and help us show praise and thanks in our daily lives. For our children and those we love, for those who entertain and those who create beauty in words and music, paint or clay,

we pray that your creative life overflow with joy.
In every place bring your hope and healing.
Lord, hear our prayer

All   **please.**

Stole and Bible

Voice   Holy God, we pray today for the life of our
church, for all who serve and all who lead.
Help us to be people who share generously
and speak boldly of your love. Give our leaders
and teachers wisdom, and give each of us the
courage we need to follow you. In every place
bring your hope and healing.
Lord, hear our prayer

All   **please.**

Mirror

Voice   Loving God, we pray for ourselves, knowing that
you see each of us with eyes of love. Help us to
love ourselves as you love us and to reflect your
image into the world around us. In my life bring
hope and healing.
Lord, hear our prayer

All   **please.**

If this is a non-eucharistic service, use the Lord's
Prayer to gather prayers together.

If a Eucharist, end prayers in usual way.

The peace

Minister   The fruit of the Spirit is love, joy, peace.
If we live in the Spirit, let us walk in the Spirit.
The peace of the Lord be always with you

All   **and also with you.** [3]

Notes

1 *New Patterns for Worship*, London: Church House Publishing, 2008, p. 96, B78.
2 *New Patterns for Worship*, p. 163, E6.
3 *New Patterns for Worship*, p. 275, H28.

 # WE GO OUT

Invite people to come and collect the gift tags. Suggest
people take them home and then attach to some
small gift to give to another person or, if your church
is going to give the harvest gifts away, they could be
attached to packets/tins before being given away.

Voice 1   We have celebrated Harvest,
brought our gifts, sung our hymns and
remembered our God.

Voice 2   As we go into the world,
may God help us to live our lives
as people of the harvest,
to share and to give,
to bless and to love,
through Jesus, our Friend and Saviour. Amen.

Blessing

Minister   May God's joy be in our hearts (*place hand
on heart*).
May God's peace be in our world (*sweep
hand out in front*).
May God's love be known between us (*hold
hands or touch palms*).
And the blessing of God,
Father, Son and Holy Spirit,
be with us, this day and always.

All   **Amen.**

The dismissal

Minister   Go in peace to love and serve the Lord.

All   **Thanks be to God.**

All Saints' Day (1 November)

Feast with friends, sing with saints

All Saints' Day falls on 1 November, and is largely irrelevant to our contemporary culture. It happens to be the day after 31 October, or Hallowe'en, now a massive event for children and families. It is also the day before 2 November – or All Souls' Day – when many churches hold annual services where people can remember those who have died, recently or long ago. This has grown significantly in recent years. However, All Saints' Day can be transferred to a Sunday or celebrated on 1 November itself, and it offers an opportunity to pick up the positive themes of light overcoming darkness and good triumphing over evil. It also looks forward with an awe-inspiring vision of eternal worship, and adds to the sense of expectation as the church year draws to an end, and we begin again waiting for the Lord to come in the season of Advent.

It may be that holding a family or children's activity day (you may even want to call it 'Holy Hallowe'en', to give the word back its proper meaning) on or near Hallowe'en, and then celebrating All Saints' Day as a church community will add significance to this season. This outline could be used on a Sunday or at a mid-week occasion, and draws on lectionary themes from the three-year cycle.

Key lectionary readings

NB: See note on lectionary readings in 'How to use this book' (p. 13).

Isaiah 25.6–9 'The heavenly banquet'
Revelation 7.9–17 'The heavenly song'
Matthew 5.1–12 'Saintly living'

Preparation

Check the church: if your church has lots of windows and memorials, prepare a checklist of names as a grid, as shown here, in this example.

Lord Montagu	Lady Montagu	Sir Percy Percy	Baby Montagu
Sybil Smythe	Captain Jones	Lady Astrid Percy	Captain Percy
St Jude	W. J. Jones	St John	Jane Smith
St Luke	Ethel Jones	St Matthew	St Mark

If your building has few memorials, you will need to place pictures and/or names of people who have been significant in the community and in the wider church around the building – those known as saints. Then prepare the grid with the checklist of names.

If you have an activity day beforehand, create life-size portraits by drawing round both adults and children present, painting and cutting out – these can be displayed in church or paraded during the service. Alternatively, make some placards or banners with names of those associated with the church.

You will need

- Copies of the checklists for everyone
- A roll of lining paper OR a small table
- A bag containing things for a special meal, e.g. plates, cups, wine, cheese, biscuits or cakes
- Prepared prayer cards, if you are using this prayer activity (see p. 82)

 ## WE GATHER

As people arrive hand them a checklist and invite them to walk around the church and complete the grid, indicating where they have found each of the people listed.

Opening hymn

This could involve a procession to include the life-size portraits if made, or several people carrying names on banners of people associated with the church. Place these around the worship space.

Informal welcome

Making ready

Suggestion: place people at different points around the church to start the echo, then repeat until everyone is joining in quietly.

Voice	The people of God are in every place
Echo	every place, every place, every place
Voice	The saints of God are in every time
Echo	every time, every time, every time
Voice	The followers of God are in every age
Echo	every age, every age, every age
Voice	In every place, every time, every age, we worship today
Echo	We worship, we worship, we worship
Voice	Today (*loudly*)
All	**Today!**

We say sorry

Making connections

Minister	One of the hallmarks of the lives of saints is that they were people of prayer and people of change. They realized that following Jesus meant living differently, and being sorry for the things that were wrong in their lives. We are also taking time now to say sorry to God for those things in our lives that have hurt other people and hurt God.
	(*Invite people very specifically to kneel (in many churches people now sit when invited to kneel). For those unable to do so, suggest clenching fists and deliberately bending arms from elbows to rest on knees.*)
Voice	Holy God, you call us to be people of prayer, but we forget to turn to you. Lord, have mercy.
All	**Lord, have mercy.**
Voice	Holy God, you call us to be people who serve, but we forget the needs of others. Christ, have mercy.

All	**Christ, have mercy.**
	(*Invite people to find a space and lie flat on the floor (for those who can't, simply ask them to place their hands flat on the seat at their sides).*)
Voice	Holy God, you call us to be people of worship, but we forget to sing your praise. Lord, have mercy.
All	**Lord, have mercy.**
Voice	Holy God, you call us to be people who love, but we forget to love you. Christ, have mercy.
All	**Christ, have mercy.**
	(*Invite all to stand.*)
Minister	May God our Father forgive *us our* sins and bring *us* to the fellowship of his table with his saints for ever.
All	**Amen.**[1]

Hymn

If the service is a Eucharist, you might like to use the Peruvian Gloria[2] or other hymn-type version.

Collect for the day or this prayer

See note on the collect or prayer for the day in 'How to use this book' (p. 14).

Minister	Holy God, across the years we hear your saints, we see their faith and hear their words as they proclaim your love; show us how to live like them, with hearts of joy and words of hope, through Jesus Christ our Lord.
All	**Amen.**

 ## WE LISTEN

Readings

Isaiah: read in usual style.

Revelation 7: see 'Additional resource: All Saints' Day' at the end of this outline (pp. 84–5) for alternative version.

Gospel: there are several alternative versions of the Beatitudes, e.g. Trevor Dennis, *The Book of Books*,[3] p. 362.

Talk

You will need to decide the theme of your banquet and use appropriate props, e.g. an afternoon tea party, a supper party or a children's party.

Either roll out the lining paper OR set up a small table and cover it with a table cloth. Ask:

> Can you see what it is yet? (It's always good to use the Rolf Harris gag!) It is a banqueting table.

Explain that this is now part of the banqueting table. Then take out from the bag various things for a feast, e.g. a napkin, plate, glass, bottle of wine, cheese and crackers OR plate, cup and saucer, cake stand with cakes on it. Say something similar to:

> The prophet Isaiah talked of how God will give a banquet for all people from all time with the best food and wine.

Ask for suggestions as to what would be there. Talk about how this represents your idea of heaven. Ask for suggestions as to what others would choose. Ask people if they can spot the problem with your table – it is only set for one.

The banquet needs guests – ask for suggestions about who will be the guests. (Suggestion: place the life-size cut-out people round the table or get others to stand around.)

> The heavenly banquet will have thousands upon thousands – the saints. All kinds of people will be there – saints are people who have chosen to follow Jesus and to serve his world. Sometimes they were – and are – attacked, ill-treated, even killed, but they carry on following Jesus. Saints are examples for us, the names we remember. They are not better or more important, just more well known.

Use the analogy of a sports team – we might know more about one or two players but the whole team is winning.

> Jesus talked about how saints would live in the reading we heard.

Ask people if they can remember any of those hallmarks. Group the hallmarks under four headings:

- Looking to Jesus, knowing they can only do things in God's strength

- Thinking about all that is good and lovely and seeing the best in human beings
- Getting upset and angry about all that is wrong in the world
- Being willing to do something about it whatever it costs

> A hallmark is something that tells others who is your maker, tells them the quality of which you are made – saints are hallmarked with Jesus.

> The banquet is timeless – it goes on and on for all eternity, always with room for everyone.

> And Revelation told one more thing – those who gather aren't just eating and drinking. They are singing God's praises for ever.

Invite the congregation to sing, e.g. 'Blessing and honour, glory and power', or to shout 'Alleluia!'.

 ## WE RESPOND

Creed or statement of faith

Making connections

Minister Let's join with God's saints from every time and place to declare the things we believe.

Use these words or other familiar form:

Minister Let us declare our faith in God.

All **We believe in God the Father,
from whom every family
in heaven and on earth is named.**

**We believe in God the Son,
who lives in our hearts through faith,
and fills us with his love.**

**We believe in God the Holy Spirit,
who strengthens us
with power from on high.**

**We believe in one God;
Father, Son and Holy Spirit.
Amen.**[4]

Prayers

Split people into small groups and give each group a prayer card with the themes and ideas for prayers. Then let people move around the church as they wish. Those who find moving difficult might choose to stay seated and visualize moving to the places as they pray.

Alternatively, if numbers are manageable, invite the whole congregation to journey with a leader to the different places in church like saints or pilgrims on a journey.

OR invite the congregation to turn to face each of the areas of the church in turn, while one or more people lead the reflection and the prayers.

Text for prayer cards

The font

The font reminds us of baptism – the beginning of the journey for every saint and for each of us. Take time to remember your own baptism and pray for those who have begun their journey of faith here in this place, praying especially for children and families:

Loving God, we thank you for calling men, women and children to follow you. We pray for everyone who has joined the journey of faith through baptism, and ask that you give them the strength and faith to keep on walking with you. Amen.

The lectern and pulpit

The lectern and pulpit remind us of hearing the word of God, of learning more of God's ways, hearing the stories of Jesus. Think about those who teach in this church, those who help us through books, through translating the Bible and through sharing their faith.

Loving God, we thank you for the gift of your word and for the gift of teaching. We pray for all those who share with others, through writing or speaking, through thinking and talking, and especially we pray for our leaders (insert local names here). Amen.

The pews/seats

These are the places where we gather as God's people, where we say sorry and listen and pray. Think about all those who gather with you here, those who come often, and those who used to be with us, and those who need to know that there is a place for them.

Loving God, we thank you for gathering us as your people. We pray for the life of our church,

and ask that you help us to pray and to serve together as we share the message of your love with those around us. Amen.

The choir stalls or music area

The saints will spend eternity praising God. Take time to pray for those who help us to worship now, who write songs and music and who lead us week by week. Think about how you worship God in your life as well as in church.

Loving God, we thank you for the gifts of music and song and dance. We pray that you give our worship leaders a spirit of joy and praise as they help us to declare your glory. Help each of us to worship you in our daily lives. Amen.

The door/porch

The door reminds us that the work of the saints is not about being inside the church but about going out into the world. Think for a moment about the needs of the world today, remembering needs in the community, the nation and the world.

Loving God, you love the world and all its people. We pray for all those in need today, especially remembering those in places of great difficulty (insert names here), asking that you bring healing and peace in every situation. Amen.

A cross

The crosses in church remind us of Jesus who has called us to follow him. Think for a few moments about all that Jesus means to you.

Loving God, thank you for Jesus. Help me to be faithful in following him each day. Amen.

The peace

Minister	God makes peace within us – let us claim it. God makes peace between us – let us share it. The peace of the Lord be with you
All	**and also with you.**[5]

If this is a Eucharist, continue with the service as usual.

Prayer D is suggested for an all-age congregation.

 ## WE GO OUT

Invite people to make a circle with their fingers, touching index fingers and thumbs together.

Repeat three times, reminding people that the halo is a sign used by artists to indicate a saint.

Voice   We remember the saints of long ago.

All   **We remember.**

Voice   We remember that we are the saints of today.

All   **We remember.**

Voice   We remember that we are surrounded by all the saints.

All   **We remember.**

Voice   We remember that we follow Jesus.

All   **We remember.**

Notes

1 *New Patterns for Worship*, London: Church House Publishing, 2008, p. 97, B83.
2 *Complete Anglican Hymns Old and New*. Stowmarket: Kevin Mayhew, 1976, 966.
3 Trevor Dennis, *The Book of Books*, Oxford: Lion Hudson, 2009, p. 362.
4 *New Patterns for Worship*, p. 166, E12.
5 The St Hilda Community, *New Women Included: A Book of Services and Prayers*, London: SPCK, 1996, p. 55.

Blessing

Minister   With the saints, know the gift of courage,
            with the saints, know the gift of faith,
            with the saints, know the gift of love.
            And the blessing of God,
            Father, Son and Holy Spirit,
            be with you all, this day and always.

All   **Amen.**

The dismissal

Minister   Go in peace to love and serve the Lord.

All   **Thanks be to God!**

John's vision from Revelation 7

This needs two voices.

Narrator   There are good dreams and there are bad dreams,
There are lovely dreams and amazing dreams,
Dreams in the night and dreams in the day,
Dreams of good and dreams of God.
A man called John had a dream,
A big, big, big, big dream,
So big we call it a vision.
The big vision needs big words,
Big pictures and big sounds
Filling our minds, flooding our hearts.
Listen . . . (whisper) listen . . .
As the dreamer John tells us more,
Speaks a revelation to us today:

John   And so the dream went on, the vision grew.
I looked and saw a huge crowd,
A crowd beyond counting,
A crowd beyond knowing,
From every nation, tribe, language, place
That has ever been known and is yet to be known.
They are standing before the throne,
The throne of God and of the Lamb, Jesus.
They are robed in white, with palm branches to wave.
Then they sing in a mighty voice,
And shout praises in a mighty song:
Blessing and honour and glory and power
Be to our God for ever and ever. Amen!*
These are the one who have struggled to the end,
These are the ones who followed Jesus
Whatever it cost, wherever they went.
Now, now they are before the throne of God.
And the promise is sure:
They will worship him day and night
And God will shelter them, keep them safe.
They will never be hungry or thirsty,

*These two lines may be sung by a choir or group.

1

Festivals Together (London: SPCK). Copyright © Sandra Millar 2012

Never be burned by the sun, or struck down by heat.
The lamb, the lamb who is Jesus
Will be their shepherd,
And he will guide them to living water, (*drop voice, pause*)
And God will wipe away all their tears.

Narrator   There are good dreams and there are bad dreams,
There are lovely dreams and amazing dreams,
Dreams in the night and dreams in the day,
Dreams of good and dreams of God.
But this is the dream of heaven.
This is John's incredible dream. (*pause*) Wow!

Remembrance Sunday

Past, present, future

Remembrance Sunday is often one of the few occasions in the church year where those gathered are truly of all ages. There will be men and women in their eighties and nineties and there will be young children from Brownies and Beavers, with a whole spread of experience in between. For many it is the only time in the year when they go inside a church, and for some young people it may be their first encounter. Yet it is a service with some serious restrictions. Rightly, there is a need for formality and respect, a seriousness of tone and a seriousness of theme, which can mean that we ignore the possibilities of creating a real encounter with God for those present.

However, it is a service where there is rich symbolism to draw on and it is also a service with clear universal themes of courage, commitment, faith and love. This outline seeks to balance valuable traditions with contemporary traditions and is based around suitable lectionary readings. It may be possible to use some of the suggestions in other contexts, such as school assembly or at a war memorial. The two-minute silence will need to be included when appropriate.

Key lectionary readings

NB: See note on lectionary readings in 'How to use this book' (p. 13).

Micah 4.1–8 'Transformed weapons'
Romans 8.31–39 'Whatever'
1 Corinthians 15.50–58 'There is a tomorrow'
OR Mark 1.14–20 'It all begins'

Preparation

You will need

- British Legion poppies; four large candles
- Photos of people (see Talk for details)
- White ribbon or strips of cloth (you may need lengths of coloured ribbon depending which prayer activity you choose)
- A tree branch
- Some war medals (if you can't find anyone present wearing any, then use pictures)

WE GATHER

As people arrive make sure everyone has access to a poppy, and hand out strips of ribbon to each person.

Opening hymn

Informal welcome

Making ready

Voice	In times of joy we hear God's word
All	**and praise his name.**
Voice	In times of pain we hear God's word
All	**and praise his name.**
Voice	In times of fear we hear God's word
All	**and praise his name.**
Voice	In every time we hear God's word
All	**and praise his name.**

We say sorry

Making connections

Minister On Remembrance Sunday we are very aware of human failure, disappointment and wrongdoing. (*Invite everyone to hold or touch the poppy they have with them*). As each candle is lit, listen to the words that express our sorrow, take time to focus on the poppy as a symbol of our sorrow . . . but also as a sign that new beginnings are always possible in God's love.

Suggestion: use different ages/voices for each section. After the person says the words, he or she turns and carries the candle to the altar, where it is lit.

Voice Loving God, you call us to love our neighbour as ourselves. But we messed it up and loved ourselves even more. (*Pause for candle to be carried forward, etc.*)
Lord, have mercy.

All **Lord, have mercy.**

Voice Loving God, you speak of peace among people and nations. But we didn't listen and let anger and hatred take root. (*Pause for candle to be carried forward, etc.*)
Christ, have mercy.

All **Christ, have mercy.**

Voice Loving God, you want justice for the poor and forgotten. But we didn't care and ignored those in need. (*Pause for candle to be carried forward, etc.*)
Lord, have mercy.

All **Lord, have mercy.**

Voice Loving God, you long for us to walk in your ways. But we didn't think and lived in selfishness and greed. (*Pause for candle to be carried forward, etc.*)
Christ, have mercy.

All **Christ, have mercy.**

Voice May God who loved the world so much that he sent his Son to be our Saviour forgive *us our* sins
and make *us* holy to serve him in the world, through Jesus Christ our Lord.

All **Amen.**[1]

Hymn

If it is a Eucharist, have the Gloria, using the traditional Peruvian Gloria[2] or other hymn-type version.

Collect for the day or this prayer

NB: Please see note on the collect or prayer for the day in 'How to use this book' (p. 14).

Voice God, our refuge and strength,
bring near the day when wars shall cease
and poverty and pain shall end,
that earth may know the peace of heaven
through Jesus Christ our Lord.

All **Amen.**[3]

 ## WE LISTEN

Readings

If possible, use the *Contemporary English Version* unless stated.

Micah: read from *The Message*. Try reading from a different place in the building, e.g. crossing, or stand up on a pew!

Romans 8: see 'Additional resource: Remembrance Sunday' at the end of this outline (pp. 91–2) for choral version with five or more voices.

Gospel: read in usual fashion using straightforward version, e.g. the *Contemporary English Version* or from the *The Lion Storyteller Bible*.

Talk

If you are involving a school, ask them to design a contemporary medal and to suggest for what it will be awarded. You can then refer to their ideas or get them to talk about their designs.

This talk can also be illustrated by a series of photos of people for each of the categories mentioned. If you use PowerPoint they could be displayed; if not simply print out and get children to parade the photos round the church.

Begin by asking people if they have any medals with them. Ask one or two to talk about why they have them. Then ask if anyone knows what the Dickin medal is for – it is awarded to animals. It is recognized as the Victoria Cross for animals. (You can find information on the Internet.) Say something similar to:

Sadie is a Labrador who has been awarded the medal for her heroism in Afghanistan. Since 1943 this medal has been given to twenty-six dogs, three horses, one cat – and thirty-two pigeons.

Show photo of medal.

It is quite surprising to discover a medal for animals!

Ask about the Elizabeth medal – given to those who have died in Afghanistan. (If appropriate, make connections with local stories or recent examples from the news. Alternatively, research real people using the Internet. You may also find that local school projects on the First or Second World War involve following the story of a real local person.) Say something similar to:

Many of those who serve in war are ordinary people whose names are never known – only a few make headlines. Harry Patch became well known a few years ago. When he died in 2009 he was the oldest veteran of the First World War – but he had never spoken of his experiences until he turned a hundred years old. Harry was simply an ordinary man doing an ordinary job who was caught up in the worst of all wars.

If possible feature some stories from the congregation and local community, e.g. 'Barbara' was 19 years old in 1945 when she joined the ATS – she worked in a shop, but decided to serve her country. She returned safely to live a full life. Show a photo of a woman in ATS.

'Stan' was a boy in 1939 living in a village in Warwickshire. His parents decided that they would welcome an evacuee child from London and two boys stayed for several months. Show a photo of a wartime child.

You could include contemporary examples or perhaps a service chaplain.

There are ordinary people who leave their homes to serve, like Harry Patch did. There are ordinary men, women and children who stay at home – some of them suffer a great deal in war and conflict. Sometimes they are persecuted for speaking out against a cruel regime.

There are people who work for peace – men, women and children who speak out, campaign or try to make a difference where they live or in a part of the world they care about.

There are people who pray – thousands of people who pray every day for those who are in the armed forces, those who live in danger and for those who work for peace.

All these people are ordinary men, women, boys and girls whose names are often only known to a few.

When Jesus called his first disciples to join him and make a difference they were just ordinary people. But they were to discover that in whatever situation they found themselves, God was always with them, helping them, encouraging them, comforting them.

Some people never get a visible medal, but the promise of God that nothing can separate us from his love is an invisible award, something that each of us can hold on to as we each continue in our own way to work for God's peace and love in the whole world.

 ## WE RESPOND

Creed or statement of faith

Making connections

Minister   Let's remember the things we share together as God' people as we declare our faith.

All   **We believe in God the Father, from whom every family in heaven and on earth is named.**

We believe in God the Son, who lives in our hearts through faith, and fills us with his love.

We believe in God the Holy Spirit, who strengthens us with power from on high.

We believe in one God; Father, Son and Holy Spirit. Amen.[4]

Prayers

In some cultures 'cotton candles' are lengths of white linen tied to tree branches to remember recent deaths. In many cultures people wear a flower or ribbon as a sign of waiting for a loved one to return. Today we are going to tie ribbons to this tree branch as a sign of our prayers for the people and situations we are thinking of. This might be an individual or it might be a nation.

EITHER

Invite people to come forward as music is played and tie their ribbon to the tree branch. During this time play suitable music, e.g. 'Where have all the flowers gone?'

Invite younger people, e.g. Scouts and Guides, to collect ribbons from those who are unable to move forward.

When everyone has done this a leader prays a gathering prayer, e.g.

Leader   Merciful God,
          surround all these we love with your care.
          Give courage in every situation where there is fear.
          Bring hope to every place where there is sorrow.
          Let there be peace in every heart and every nation
          and keep each of us close to your heart.
          In Jesus' name we pray.
          Amen.

OR

Invite people to hold their ribbon or tie it to a finger as the prayers are read.

Then, collect the ribbons during the offertory and have them tied to the tree branch OR invite people to bring ribbons with them during communion and tie them to the branch before returning to their seats.

During each section someone holds up a ribbon of the appropriate colour.

Voice   White is the colour of peace, the colour of new beginnings, the colour of purity.
          We pray for countries where peace is a fragile new beginning, remembering (*name current situations here*). Give purity of heart to those who lead that they may do so with integrity and justice for all people.
          Lord, in your mercy

All   **hear our prayer.**

Voice   Red is the colour of anger, the colour of bloodshed, the colour of love.
          We pray for places where there is violence and war, remembering those who are serving with the armed forces, those who are working to bring help and those who are speaking for peace. Give all who serve a heart of compassion so that hatred may turn to love.
          Lord, in your mercy

All   **hear our prayer.**

Voice   Green is the colour of life, the colour of growth, the colour of hope.
          We pray for community life everywhere, especially for children and young people, and we remember all those who work to foster life and health in whatever way. Give all who are in need of healing and new beginnings a sense of hope so that vision and purpose may be renewed.
          Lord, in your mercy

All   **hear our prayer.**

Voice   Yellow is the colour of warmth, the colour of energy, the colour of joy.
          We give thanks today for every blessing in our lives – for comrades and friends, for work and leisure, for food and homes – for all that brings us delight. We pray for all who share our daily lives with us, and ask that you stir up joy and gladness in our hearts that we might bring glory to your name.
          Lord, in your mercy

All   **hear our prayer.**

Voice   Brown is the colour of building, the colour of foundations, the colour of faith.
          We give thanks today for this building and for the life of the Church throughout the world.
          We pray for all who minister in your name and ask that you help each of us to hold fast to that which is good, to share your love and to be faithful in your service.
          (*End prayers with familiar formal ending, e.g.*)
          Merciful Father, accept these prayers for the sake of your Son, our Saviour, Jesus Christ.
          Amen.[5]

The peace

Minister God makes peace within us – let us claim it.
          God makes peace between us – let us share it.
          The peace of the Lord be with you

All   **and also with you.**[6]

If this is a Eucharist, continue with the service as usual. Prayer D ('This is our story, this is our song') is suggested for use with an all-age congregation.

➡ WE GO OUT

Notices may be included at this point as part of moving the focus to our Christian lives.

Blessing

Minister May God's joy be in our hearts (*place hand on heart*).
May God's peace be in our world (*sweep hand out in front*).
May God's love be known between us (*hold hands or touch palms*).
And the blessing of God,

Father, Son and Holy Spirit,
be with us, this day and always.

All **Amen.**

The dismissal

Minister Go in peace to love and serve the Lord.

All **Thanks be to God.**

Notes

1 *New Patterns for Worship*, London: Church House Publishing, 2008, p. 97, B82.
2 *Complete Anglican Hymns Old and New*, Stowmarket: Kevin Mayhew, 1976, 966.
3 *Common Worship: Additional Collects*, London: Church House Publishing, 2004, p. 25.
4 *New Patterns for Worship*, p. 166, E12.
5 *Common Worship: Services and Prayers for the Church of England*, London: Church House Publishing, 2000, p. 174.
6 The St Hilda Community, *New Women Included: A Book of Services and Prayers*, London: SPCK, 1996, p. 55.

Whatever

A reading based on Romans 8.31–39

This needs rehearsing to do it well. You will need one main voice and a chorus with a minimum of four voices.

Voice   Listen, folks! If God is for us, who is against us?

Chorus Who is against us?

Voice   For God sent his Son,

Chorus even his Son,

Voice   and gave him for all of us,

Chorus all of us, all of you, all of us, all of you. (*softer voices, actions*)

Voice   So won't this God meet our every need, give us everything else?

Chorus Meeting our every need in every way?

Voice   Who can say anything against God's special people?

Chorus Who could? Who could say anything?

Voice   Because it is God who is with us,

Chorus God is with us. God is with us.

Voice   It is Jesus who died,

Chorus Jesus who lives,

Voice   Jesus at the right hand of God,

Chorus who is praying for us, for us, for us! (*getting louder*)

Voice   Who will separate us from the love of Jesus?

Chorus Will hard times?

Voice   Troubled times?

Chorus Hatred or hunger or homelessness?

Voice   Danger, threats, difficulties?

Chorus Will any of this separate us from the love of Jesus?

Voice   NO!

Chorus No! For we are more than conquerors,

Voice   more than conquerors in Jesus who loved us.

Chorus So . . . so . . . so . . . neither (*next section said quickly, as a ball tossed back and forth*)

Voice   death

Chorus nor life

1

Voice   nor angels

Chorus   nor rulers

Voice   nor things happening now

Chorus   nor things yet to come

Voice   not height

Chorus   not depth

Voice   not anything else in all creation

Chorus   not anything at all in all the world

Voice   will be able to separate us (*slower*)

Chorus   us, you, me, US

Voice   from the love of God

All   in Christ Jesus our Lord! Amen!

Festivals Together (London: SPCK). From Sandra Millar, *Resourcing November*, Gloucester: Jumping Fish, 2009, p. 16.
Copyright © Sandra Millar 2009, 2012

St Nicholas (6 December)

Children for a change

Unless your church is named after St Nicholas, it's unlikely you will have celebrated this as a festival. But it's a great opportunity to focus on children and families, and might make part of a special event during the approach to Christmas. As this feast falls right in the middle of the Advent season, it would work as an additional service to the principal Sunday morning Eucharist or could be part of a mid-week celebration. It is also an opportunity to involve children in leading and taking part as indicated. However, it could also be used in churches where there are few or no children actively involved, as a reminder that children are an essential part of God's family.

Key lectionary readings

NB: Please see note on lectionary readings in 'How to use this book' (p. 13).

Advent is a season that requires the set lectionary readings for the day in a Church of England principal service.

Isaiah 6.1–8 'Willing and able'
1 Timothy 4.11–16 'Young leadership'
Mark 10.13–16 'Children welcome'

Preparation

If you are able to set up a series of activities for people to do as an alternative way of exploring the word, you will need to make sure that you have these materials:

- Handbells
- A large roll of wallpaper
- A variety of collage materials
- Fabric squares and fabric paints
- Ribbon to join the squares together (a pre-made version is available through Baker Ross and other similar suppliers)
- Paper, scissors and colouring materials
- Thin gold card to make cones
- Glue
- Sweets
- People-shaped keyrings (also available from craft suppliers)
- Paints
- Cones filled with sweets to give away (if not made in the activity)

 WE GATHER

Opening hymn

Informal welcome

Formal introduction

Minister   The Lord be with you
All   **and also with you.**

Invite all the children present to go and find an adult and together make a circle inside the church. (This might have to be an approximation, especially in small churches with only one aisle and fixed pews – but it can be done!)

When everyone is in place:

Voice	We are the family of God.
All	**We are the family of God.**
Voice	We are the people of God.
All	**We are the people of God.**
Voice	We are the children of God.
All	**We are the children of God.**
Voice	We will praise his name.
All	**We will praise his name.**
Voice	We will hear his word.
All	**We will hear his word.**
Voice	We will meet him here.
All	**We will meet him here.** **We will!**
Voice	This is the day that the Lord has made. We will rejoice and be glad in it. Inspire us in our worship, stretch us in our thinking, and change us in our lives. Amen.

You may like to accompany the Amen with high fives all round before returning to seats.

We say sorry

Making connections

Invite children and younger adults to the front.

Minister	Today is an opportunity to think about how we treat children in the Church and the world, and how we treat each other.

Children are used to raising a hand in answer to a question, so after each question, invite everyone to raise a hand and say: 'We are.'

Voice	*Children and adults* are you sorry that as part of the Church you have not always taken children seriously and welcomed them fully in Jesus' name?
All	**We are.**
Voice	Lord God, forgive us for neglecting children in our worship and our mission. Lord, have mercy.
All	**Lord, have mercy.**
Voice	*Children and adults* are you sorry for all the times you have ignored or disobeyed parents and others who have tried to help and support you?
All	**We are.**

Voice	Lord God, forgive us for not listening to others and not doing what we should. Christ, have mercy.
All	**Christ, have mercy.**
Voice	*Children and adults* are you sorry for forgetting to follow Jesus and live his way at home, at school, at work, with friends, with strangers?
All	**We are.**
Voice	Lord God, forgive us for ignoring you and going our own way. Lord, have mercy.
All	**Lord, have mercy.**
Minister	May the God of love and power forgive *us* and free *us* from *our* sins, heal and strengthen *us* by his Spirit, and raise *us* to new life in Christ our Lord.
All	**Amen.**[1]

Hymn/Gloria

Collect for the day or this prayer

NB: Please see note on the collect or prayer for the day in 'How to use this book' (p. 14).

Minister	Jesus, child of Mary, light from God, help us to share the gifts of children, to recognize that every child matters, and bring hope to children in need, so that every man, woman and child may know your blessing and shine as lights in the world to the glory of God.
All	**Amen.**[2]

 ## WE LISTEN

Reading(s)

Isaiah: try reading from a different place in the building, e.g. crossing, or stand up on a pew or window sill. Unroll a scroll and proclaim the message. Invite children to ring handbells and shout: 'Oyez! Oyez! Listen to the prophet!'

1 Timothy: See 'Additional resource: St Nicholas' at the end of this outline (p. 97) for version to read with children and adults.

Gospel: invite children to read.

Talk

If your church is able, offer a series of activities instead of a talk. Set up the activities at various points around the church and encourage people to choose one or more to do in the time available.

Activities

- Create a collage with images of happy and sad children from across the world. Caption it 'Children matter'.
- Design fabric squares for each person which join together to make a banner.
- Make and decorate paper planes.
- Make small paper cones and fill with raisins or sweets.
- Decorate people-shaped key rings.
- Discuss in a group how children can be more involved in the life of the church using the readings as a starting point.

When the time is up, return to seats. Talk briefly about each object, reminding people that St Nicholas responded to God's call as a young man. Say something similar to:

> The collage reminds us that there are billions of children in the world today – often playing and smiling in difficult circumstances. Jesus told us to be like them, learn from them – play more, smile more, love more.
>
> Everyone of every age has a place in God's family – yet each person is also special, with a unique call from God. The planes remind us of the hopes we have, the ideas we have that will make a difference to our world. The readings reminded us that God calls at every age, and that even young people can take on leadership.
>
> The cones are gifts to give away, reminding us of St Nicholas, and reminding us that we are family together, learning from one another, and growing together in God's love.

OR

Simply invite a volunteer to come out to the front and stand next to you.

If there is a young child present, this is almost certainly the person who will come forward!

(If there are no children present, or they are too small, then the chances are no one will move.)

When the volunteer gets to the front, simply give them a treat and lots of praise, then send them back to their seat.

Draw attention to the fact that a child took a risk or, if no child is present, talk about why adults can't take risks any more. Children are willing to try things, have adventures, explore and discover the world. They take joy in possibilities and the belief that it is possible to do things differently.

Talk about the *Blue Peter* appeal each year that raises lots of money. Talk about how children get involved with Children in Need. Talk about how young leaders speak up for things, e.g. Iqbal Masih (see the 2013 film *The Carpet Boy*), who spoke all over the world on behalf of child labourers.

> The reading from Isaiah reminds us that God's call to play a part in changing the world is not dependent on how good or worthy we are, but simply on God's call. St Paul writes to encourage Timothy, a young leader, and St Nicholas was also called by God at only twelve years old. Jesus also reminds us that children need to be welcomed and blessed and in turn will be a blessing to all of us.

Encourage people to pray for children.

 ## WE RESPOND

Creed or statement of faith

Suggest that this might be introduced by a child.

Making connections

Minister Let's remind ourselves that we all belong to the same family of God:

All **We believe in God the Father,
from whom every family
in heaven and on earth is named.**

**We believe in God the Son,
who lives in our hearts through faith,
and fills us with his love.**

**We believe in God the Holy Spirit,
who strengthens us
with power from on high.**

**We believe in one God;
Father, Son and Holy Spirit.
Amen.**[3]

Prayers

The actions in these prayers can be done either literally or imaginatively.

Invite people to stand and use both arms to make a very large circle in front of themselves. Make the circle several times.

Voice   Loving God, we remember all the children of the world. You know and care for each one, those who are happy and those who are sad. We pray especially for children who are hungry and homeless, frightened or alone. We pray for all those who are working to help make a difference.
Lord, hear our prayer

All   **please.**

(Invite people to use one hand to make a circle in front of themselves.)

Voice   Loving God, we remember all the children in our community. We pray for all those places where children go, our schools, playgroups, churches, surgeries, leisure centres. We ask you to help children learn well and play well, and ask you to give wisdom to those who help them.
Lord, hear our prayer

All   **please.**

(Invite people to use one hand to make a circle the size of their face.)

Voice   Loving God, we pray for those children we know well, our families and our friends. We pray for families in difficulties and ask that you help them to know your peace.
Lord, hear our prayer

All   **please.**

(Invite people to make a small circle using finger and thumb.)

Voice   Loving God, we pray for ourselves, and ask you to help us follow you more closely each day.

Help each one of us to remember that every person of every age is special and to share your love with those we meet.
Lord, hear our prayer

All   **please.**

If the service is a service of the word, it might be a good idea to end the prayers with the Lord's Prayer, before sharing the peace together.

If the service is a Eucharist, continue with the peace followed by the offertory and the eucharistic prayer. Involve different generations as appropriate.

The peace

Introduce the peace, using these or similar words:

Minister   God makes peace within us – let us claim it.
God makes peace between us – let us share it.
The peace of the Lord be with you

All   **and also with you.**[4]

 # WE GO OUT

Notices may be included at this point as part of moving the focus to our Christian lives.

Either hand out the cones with sweets made earlier or simply hand out sweets.

Voice   Let's go into the world to live as God's children,
to share with God's children,
to play like God's children,
to love all God's world.

Invite people to skip or dance out during the final hymn or organ recessional.

Blessing

Minister   May the peace of Jesus be in your hearts,
may the joy of Jesus be on your lips,
may the hope of Jesus be in your life,
and the blessing of God,
Father, Son and Holy Spirit,
be with you this day and always.

All   **Amen.**

Notes

1 *New Patterns for Worship*, London: Church House Publishing, 2008, p. 97, B80.
2 A prayer specially written for the 2009 Year of the Child, in Sandra Millar, *Resourcing November*, Gloucester: Jumping Fish, 2009, p. 35.
3 *New Patterns for Worship*, p. 166, E12.
4 The St Hilda Community, *New Women Included: A Book of Services and Prayers*, London: SPCK, 1996, p. 55.

A reading of 1 Timothy 4.11–16

Suggestion for the lines below: an adult reads the words in smaller print, and the words in larger print are read from the front by two/three children. There could be additional young readers standing up among the congregation, so that several voices say these lines together.

Adult Teach these things and insist that everyone learn them. Don't let anyone look down on you because you are young.

Children **No, no one should look down on us because we are young.**

Adult Be an example to all believers in what you say, in the way you live, in your love, your faith, and your purity.

Children **We can be an example in words, actions, love, faith and the good choices we make.**

Adult Until I get there, focus on reading the Scriptures to the church, encouraging the believers, and teaching them.

Children **We can share God's word, encourage other people, even teach them.**

Adult Do not neglect the spiritual gift you received through the prophecy spoken over you when the elders of the church laid their hands on you.

Children **We won't reject or neglect the gifts we have, ours from our baptism.**

Adult Give your complete attention to these matters. Throw yourself into your tasks so that everyone will see your progress.

Children **We will commit ourselves to walking in God's ways. The whole church will see us grow.**

Adult Keep a close watch on how you live and on your teaching.

Children **We will guard our souls, our words and our actions.**

Adult Stay true to what is right for the sake of your own salvation and the salvation of those who hear you.

Children **We will stay true to Jesus and bring God's salvation to the world.**

Festivals Together (London: SPCK). Copyright © Sandra Millar 2012

Christmas Day

No time like the present

Some churches have a strong tradition of family attendance on Christmas Day, while others seem to have a small gathering of regulars. There may also be visitors present, some familiar with church, others not. Whatever group are present, the challenge is to offer something new as people go into a day of celebration. This outline encourages people to remember that Christmas is a season, not just a day.

Key lectionary readings

NB: Please see note on lectionary readings in 'How to use this book' (p. 13).

Christmas is a season that requires the set lectionary readings for the day in a Church of England principal service.

Isaiah 52.7–10 'It's good news!'
Titus 3.4–7 'God comes to save'
Luke 2.1–20 'The big story'

Preparation

You will need

- People dressed up as characters from the nativity story (angel, innkeeper, shepherd) or pictures to hold or display on screen
- Handbells or trumpet
- A mock calendar showing Christmas Day and twelve more days underneath (a sketch book or flip chart would work)
- Presents to look at
- A baby doll in a plastic crate

WE GATHER

Opening hymn

Informal welcome

Formal introduction

Minister	The Lord be with you
All	**and also with you.**
	(Spread hands into star shapes and wiggle as if twinkling. Stretch up high and make actions.)
Voice	Starshine in the night, lead us to Jesus.
All	**Lead us to Jesus.**
	(Reach out at shoulder height and make star actions.)
Voice	Starshine on this day, lead us to Jesus.
All	**Lead us to Jesus.**
	(Place hands over heart and make star actions.)
Voice	Starshine in our hearts, lead us to Jesus.
All	**Lead us to Jesus.**

We say sorry

Voice	'When the goodness of God appeared, he saved us.'
Minister	That's what today is about: God's goodness and love shown to everyone. But we sometimes forget that. Let's pause and remember the times we have let God down.

Either show pictures on a screen or dress up three figures (as an angel, innkeeper and shepherd) to walk down the nave during these prayers.

NB: In churches other than the Church of England, each section could end with this response:

Voice	Forgive us, Lord.
All	**Forgive us.**

(Church of England churches should use an authorized confession:)

Angel	The angels sang praises to God and filled the sky with song. But we forget to give God thanks for all the good things in our lives. Lord, have mercy.
All	**Lord, have mercy.**
Innkeeper	The innkeeper made room for Mary and Joseph and Jesus was born safely. But we fill our lives with so much that there is no room for Jesus. Christ, have mercy.
All	**Christ, have mercy.**
Shepherd	The shepherds went quickly to see the child in the manger. But we are so busy and so selfish that we forget to tell others the good news. Lord, have mercy.
All	**Lord, have mercy.**
Minister	May God who loved the world so much that he sent his Son to be our Saviour forgive *us our* sins and make *us* holy to serve him in the world, through Jesus Christ our Lord.
All	**Amen.**[1]

Hymn/Gloria

Collect for the day or this prayer

NB: Please see note on the collect or prayer for the day in 'How to use this book' (p. 14).

Voice	Lord Jesus Christ, your birth at Bethlehem draws us to kneel in wonder at heaven touching earth: accept our heartfelt praise as we worship you, our Saviour and our eternal God.
All	**Amen.**[2]

 ## WE LISTEN

Reading(s)

Isaiah: try reading from a different place, e.g. crossing, or stand up on a pew or window sill. Unroll a scroll and proclaim the message.

Titus: read from a version such as *The Message*.

Gospel: this is one of those occasions when it would be very effective to 'proclaim' the Gospel from memory. This allows the reader to move about, make eye contact and add a 'story' dimension. Make the acclamation really joyful with handbells or trumpet to accompany.

Talk

Hold up a large calendar showing 25 December (underneath have twelve more days marked as Christmas). Say something similar to:

> Everyone knows what day it is today.

Ask what clues there are – look at some of the presents, which seem to be one of the clues.

Then invite everyone to do some time travel – by standing up and walking backwards on the spot.

Explain that we have travelled back 2,000 years. Ask how we know what day it is.

Point to the baby in the manger (or place a doll in plastic crate at one side).

> A baby had been born. Thousands of babies were born every day. Mostly we have no idea whether a baby is going to be a special person when he or she grows up (although every baby is special – just ask some grandparents!). Just occasionally there are clues.

Ask for ideas what kind of clues we might have.

> Sometimes it is because the parents are already famous or powerful – not the case with Mary and Joseph.

> But sometimes it's because someone has said something, which is what had happened to Mary and Joseph and the shepherds. They had a clue that this was a special day. They had been told the baby was a gift from God.

> Now some gifts can be used straight away.

Ask people if they have already eaten any presents or used them up.

> Other gifts last a bit longer, maybe even a lifetime.

Ask if anyone has a present from many years ago that they are still using or wearing.

> But God's gift was not just for a day, not even for a few years.

> God's gift of a baby was a beginning, the beginning of something that would last for ever.

Invite people to begin time travel movement in reverse . . . Say that for a hundred, two hundred, five hundred, a thousand, fifteen hundred, two thousand years, people have been discovering the meaning of God's gift that day.

Point to the date again.

Christmas day is not the end. It's just a beginning. We can still discover the meaning of this gift from God for the next twelve days (*rip off the rest of the calendar*) and then for all of our lives.

Christmas: the birth of Jesus, God's gift for all time.

 WE RESPOND

Creed or statement of faith

Making connections

Minister Let's remind ourselves that we all belong to the same family of God:

All **We believe in God the Father,**
from whom every family
in heaven and on earth is named.

We believe in God the Son,
who lives in our hearts through faith,
and fills us with his love.

We believe in God the Holy Spirit,
who strengthens us
with power from on high.

We believe in one God;
Father, Son and Holy Spirit.
Amen.[3]

Prayers

These prayers have a sung refrain, based on a well-known carol.

Invite everyone to look up to the roof, and imagine the sky above full of angels singing with a message of good news for the world. Pray using these or similar words:

Voice Loving God, we listen again to the message of the angels and we pray for our world today. Help us to be people who tell others of your love. We pray for all those who help us to sing your praises and who help us understand the gift you have given us in Jesus.

All sing **Hark the herald angels sing, glory to the newborn king.**

(*Invite everyone to look out through the windows, and imagine the shepherds on the hillside listening and then walking towards the stable.*)

Voice Loving God, we watch again as the shepherds hurry to the manger and we pray for our world today. Help us to be people who welcome everyone into our midst. We pray for those who feel alone and afraid today, and for those who will come alongside to help.

All sing **Hark the herald angels sing, glory to the newborn king.**

(*Invite everyone to turn towards the door, and imagine the wise men far away looking into the sky and preparing gifts to bring.*)

Voice Loving God, we look again as the wise men prepare to journey, and we pray for our world today. Help us to be people who long to know more about you. We pray for all those who teach others and all who discover new things. We ask that you will help us to be people with open hearts and minds.

All sing **Hark the herald angels sing, glory to the newborn king.**

(*Invite everyone to turn to the front, and to look down towards the floor, and imagine Mary and Joseph in the stable, gazing at the baby.*)

Voice Loving God, we come close again to Mary and Joseph, and we pray for our world today. Help us to be people who come close to you. We pray for families and friends coming close to each other today, and remember those who may be torn apart. We ask that you help each of us to learn more about loving you and loving one another.

All sing **Hark the herald angels sing, glory to the newborn king.**

(*Invite everyone to look into their lap, and imagine they are looking at Jesus in the manger. Invite people to be still for a moment and make their own prayer.*
End with this prayer or by singing 'Glory to the newborn king'.)

Voice Jesus, Saviour, child of Mary,
you know us and love us,
you share our lives
and hear our prayer.
Glory to you for ever. Amen.

The peace

The minister introduces the peace, using these or similar words.

Minister Unto us a child is born, unto us a son is given, and his name shall be called the Prince of Peace. The peace of the Lord be with you

All **and also with you.**[4]

 # WE GO OUT

Notices may be included at this point as part of moving the focus to our Christian lives.

Blessing

Voice God sent his angels from glory to bring to shepherds the good news of Jesus' birth.

All **Amen. We thank you, Lord.**

Voice You have heard his story, the story of God's own Son.

All **Amen. We thank you, Lord.**

Voice May he fill you with joy to bring this good news to others today.

All **Amen. We thank you, Lord.**[5]

Minister And the blessing of God, the Father, Son and Holy Spirit be with you and those you love, this day and always.

All **Amen.**

Minister Go in peace to love and serve the Lord.

All **In the name of Christ. Amen.**

Notes

1 *New Patterns for Worship*, London: Church House Publishing, 2008, p. 97, B82.
2 *Common Worship: Additional Collects*, London: Church House Publishing, 2004, p. 6.
3 *New Patterns for Worship*, p. 166, E12.
4 *New Patterns for Worship*, p. 273, H15.
5 *Common Worship: Times and Seasons*, London: Church House Publishing, 2006, p. 101, P8.

Patronal/dedication festival or special event

The heart of everything

During the course of a year there may be other opportunities for a festival celebration. It may link in with a community tradition such as a feast day or the arrival of the travelling fair, or it may be that there is a national event that offers a reason for celebration.

Alongside this there are also moments when the local church can celebrate its own unique story. Some churches have a tradition of celebrating a patronal festival, that is holding a special service on or near the feast day of the saint after which the church is named. Depending on the particular patron saint, this might give rise to a wealth of fascinating themes, symbols and stories, or it might present a challenge!

There is also the possibility of a dedication festival, which commemorates the actual opening of the church. For many churches there is a definite beginning that can be celebrated. But even if you don't know the exact date and year, the annual calendar allows for a dedication festival to be celebrated on the first Sunday in October or the last Sunday after Trinity. Whenever you celebrate, this is a great occasion to include all ages and to welcome those on the edge of church life.

This outline takes a central theme of love, the love that lies at the beginning of every Christian life and every Christian project. You will need to add local interest and appropriate readings to reflect your church and community. You might also want to add a procession through the community carrying banners or objects that tell the story of your church/saint.

Readings

Genesis 28.10–18 'Joining heaven and earth'
Psalm 122 'Welcome to Jerusalem'
Ephesians 2 'It's about people'
Luke 15.11–24 (25–31) 'It's love that brings us back'

Preparation

You will need

- Lengths of coloured fabric: green, rust/brown; yellow; indigo; red; and a long length (6 metres or so) of white folded into a gift box (sheer fabrics work well)
- Bookmarks with suggested verse and picture of church/saint

 ## WE GATHER

Opening hymn

Informal welcome

Making ready

Voice 1	I was glad, yes I was, when they said: 'Let's go, let's go, let's go to the house of God!'
Voice 2	I am glad, yes I am, when I go, when I go, when I go, into the house of God.
	(*With appropriate accompanying actions.*)
Voice 1	God of small things – we love you (*pinch fingers almost together*)
All	**and praise your name** (*punch air with right hand*).
Voice 2	God of huge things – we love you (*stretch one hand as far as possible in front of other*)

All	**and praise your name.**
Voice 1	God of amazing things – we love you (*twirl forefinger outwards from forehead in circles*).
All	**and praise your name.**
Voice 2	God of everything – we love you (*make large circle with arms*)
All	**and praise your name.**

We say sorry

Making connections

Minister	God has given each of us so much to enjoy in our lives and given us so much to share. But sometimes we become selfish and mean. We remember the times we have let God down and ask for forgiveness. (*Touch hands to head.*)
Voice	Lord God, forgive us for thinking too much about ourselves. Forgive us for not using our minds to think of others. Lord, have mercy.
All	**Lord, have mercy.** (*Touch hands to ears.*)
Voice	Lord God, forgive us for not paying attention to other people. Forgive us for listening to things that harm us and others. Christ, have mercy.
All	**Christ, have mercy.** (*Touch hands to lips.*)
Voice	Lord God, forgive us for speaking carelessly. Forgive us for staying silent when we should speak out. Lord, have mercy.
All	**Lord, have mercy.** (*Touch hands to shoulders.*)
Voice	Lord God, forgive us for not helping other people in their lives. Forgive us for not sharing our own needs with others. Christ, have mercy.
All	**Christ, have mercy.** (*Touch one hand to another.*)
Voice	Lord God, forgive us for holding tight to things we should give away. Forgive us for letting go of things we should take care of. Lord, have mercy.

All	**Lord, have mercy.** (*Touch hands to knees.*)
Voice	Lord God, forgive us for forgetting to say thank you in prayer. Forgive us for thinking we are not important. Christ, have mercy.
All	**Christ, have mercy.** (*Touch hands to feet.*)
Voice	Lord God, forgive us for doing nothing. Forgive us for walking away from you. Lord, have mercy.
All	**Lord, have mercy.** (*Touch hands to heart.*)
Voice	Lord God, forgive us for all that we do wrong and for the wrong in your world.
Minister	May the God of love bring *us* back to himself, forgive *us our* sins, and assure *us* of his eternal love in Jesus Christ our Lord.
All	**Amen.**[1]

Hymn/Gloria

Use traditional Peruvian[2] or other hymn type of Gloria.

Collect for the day or this prayer

NB: Please see note on the collect or prayer for the day in 'How to use this book' (p. 14).

Voice	Faithful God, you inspire your people to follow you and give them courage to do something new; keep us full of faith and hope that we too might show love in this place, through Jesus Christ our Saviour.
All	**Amen.**

 WE LISTEN

Readings

Genesis 28: mini-drama (see 'Additional resource: dedication festival' at the end of this outline (p. 107).

Ephesians: read from a contemporary version (see 'How to use this book', p. 14, and 'Biblical and other resources', p. 108, for suggestions).

Gospel: the presentation of the Gospel reading is the talk. If the service is a Eucharist, it could still be started with an acclamation, then presented creatively as indicated in the talk up to the beginning of the discussion. If appropriate, follow with a formal reading of the text before the discussion and reflection.

It is important that the creative presentation comes before the formal story is told.

Talk

Make sure the coloured fabrics can be seen – the chancel step might be okay if it's visible, or place a chair or table at the front. I have also found it effective to drape/tie the fabrics from the pulpit or over the altar.

You will have to put into a bag (in this order starting from the bottom): red fabric, indigo, yellow, rust/brown, green, and the box containing the white fabric on the top.

Begin by removing the box. Do not open it: ask what people think it contains; act as if it is heavy; listen carefully to it and invite others to do so. Then place it to one side, saying that it turns out this story will be about a gift.

Bring out the green fabric. Ask what green makes people think about – grass, parks, summer, etc. For today, it represents a field.

The field is on a farm. The story takes place on a farm, where a man lives with his two sons. Say something similar to:

> One of the sons looks around the green fields of the farm and thinks to himself, this is boring, this is dull, this is all the same every day. He looks into the distance and thinks he can see bright lights, life, colour and energy. 'Let me go there,' he asks his dad. 'Give me the money I would have if you were dead and let me go!' His dad agrees, and gives him all the money.

Lay out the rust/brown fabric as a kind of road.

> So the young man journeyed away from the farm to where he could see the bright lights of the city.

Bring out the yellow fabric. Ask people what yellow makes them think of – sun, happiness, holidays and . . .

> Yes, it seemed like every day was a holiday, every day the sun shone. He found loads of mates, had loads of fun, spent loads of money. It was fantastic!

> Then one day he went to get some more money – and nothing! There was nothing left.

> Suddenly the young man found that all his friends were nothing too. There was no one hanging around now, no one to lend him money or give him a bed or even a snack.

Pull out the indigo fabric and curl it into a ball. As you do so, ask what it makes them think of – misery, sadness, despair. Place it on the yellow.

> It was all those things. The young man was in a very, very hard place. The only work he could find was feeding pigs, and the only food was the food given for pigs – stuff like we put out to recycle! It was horrible, and he found himself remembering the dull green farm.

> Even the servants have more to eat than this, he thought. I'll go back and see if my dad will give me a job, any job.

Take out the colour red – discuss what it might mean – blood and anger, danger.

> And yes, the young man thought that when he met his father, the father would be filled with anger, would maybe warn him away from the farm, even hit him! So he drew close with a heart full of fear.

> But as he drew near, the father began to run down the path . . . because the young man had forgotten that red is also the colour of love. The father loved his son so much, he waited every day for him to come home. He ran to him and wrapped his arms round him. 'I've missed you so much!' he cried. 'I'm so glad that you are home . . .'

> And he handed him a present.

Pick up the box. Lift a corner of the lid and hand one corner of the fabric to a volunteer who needs to walk backwards pulling the fabric slowly. (If you have arranged it properly, it will fall gently from the box.)

> What does white make us think of? Doves, weddings, snow, maybe water.

> White is the sign of something pure and new. The father gave the son the gift of a new start, the gift of love, the beginning of a new life.

If you want to continue with the story, simply add that the older brother was angry and complained.

> He was angry. He didn't feel the same love – until the father reminded him that he had always been able to enjoy the farm; he always knew the father's love. Who knows, maybe that was a new beginning for the older brother too.

Discuss the story together. Talk about how every Christian's story begins with a moment of knowing that God offers a new start. If it's a patronal festival, talk about your saint and his or her story and how, after discovering God's love, he or she began to serve and share with others.

If it's a dedication festival, you might talk about what inspired local Christians to build the church and how it is a place that is always offering the chance of a new start, whatever we have done, however much we have forgotten God's love.

 WE RESPOND

Creed or statement of faith

NB: It may be appropriate on this occasion to use the formal Apostles' Creed.

Making connections

Minister   Let's declare our faith, just as people have done for years/centuries in this place:

All   **We believe in God the Father,
from whom every family
in heaven and on earth is named.**

**We believe in God the Son,
who lives in our hearts through faith,
and fills us with his love.**

**We believe in God the Holy Spirit,
who strengthens us
with power from on high.**

**We believe in one God;
Father, Son and Holy Spirit.
Amen.**[3]

Prayers

These prayers are an imaginative journey around the world. It works well to use one person to do the 'travel meditation' and a different voice to offer the formal prayer. Use these or similar words.

Invite everyone to stand and turn to their left (which should be north, but might not actually be north, so these are 'symbolic directions').

Face north

Talk about the things that lie beyond that window in your community, then imagine travelling across to Scotland, the North Sea and all the way to the Arctic Circle. Think about the adventure of going to explore unknown places and think about the environment and our greed in creation that damages the earth. Thank God for the abundance and variety of the world.

Voice   Dear God, we thank you for the wonder of creation, and the joy of living in this place. We pray today for all who work to understand our world and we remember especially those who work in and for our local community. We pray for those who work for little reward to bring us the things we enjoy, and ask that you help us to act for change.
God of hope, in your mercy

All   **hear our prayer.**

Turn left again to face the back of the church (west)

If the font is there, start by praying for families, and children. Then travel in your mind to the west, across Wales, across the ocean to the great continents of the Americas – Canada, South America and the USA, where so many world organizations are based:

Voice   Dear God, we pray for those who hold power and influence in our world, especially remembering the United Nations and others who try to bring peace and healing. Help all in government and authority to act with integrity and righteousness, and give them courage to speak for those who are vulnerable, especially children and families.
God of peace, in your mercy

All   **hear our prayer.**

Turn left again (south)

Talk about the things that lie beyond this wall in your community. Travel south in your mind, perhaps remembering holidays at the sea in this country, Europe, the Mediterranean, then the great continent of Africa with so much diversity, so much beauty, so many gifts to offer us, and yet so many people in need.

Voice Dear God, we pray for those who struggle to bring about healing in the world, whether for individuals or for communities. Give them wisdom and skill and help us to learn together in our world so that every man, woman and child may live in security and peace. We remember today those who are struggling in our parishes or families, and pray that your light will shine in their shadows.
God of love, in your mercy

All **hear our prayer.**

Turn towards the front (east)

Facing the altar, talk about God and his people, pray for the local church, spreading out across the diocese. As we travel beyond the walls towards the east, we find some of the greatest populations of the world – and some of its most troubled places.

Voice Dear God, we give thanks today for those who have worshipped in this place for generations. We pray for our bishops, for our church leaders and for all who minister your love, that we may have confidence to speak the good news with joy. We remember all churches that are struggling, for whatever reason, and ask that your presence will draw close today.
God of joy, in your mercy

All **hear our prayer.**

Finally, invite people to stand still, placing hands on hearts.

Voice Dear God, we pray for ourselves and those close to our own hearts today.

We ask you to keep us walking with you, help us to continue hearing your word and sharing your love with those in need.

All **Amen.**

Notes

1 *New Patterns for Worship*, London: Church House Publishing, 2008, p. 95, B73.
2 *Complete Anglican Hymns Old and New*, Stowmarket: Kevin Mayhew, 1976, 966.
3 *New Patterns for Worship*, p. 166, E12.
4 The St Hilda Community, *New Woman Included: A Book of Services and Prayers*, London: SPCK, 1996, p. 55.

The peace

Minister God makes peace within us – let us claim it. God makes peace between us – let us share it. The peace of the Lord be with you

All **and also with you.**[4]

If this is a Eucharist, continue with the service as usual. Use Prayer D ('This is our story, this is our song') for an all-age congregation.

 # WE GO OUT

Suggestion: give out a prayer card/bookmark with a photo of the church or a saint, and encourage everyone to give thanks for what has been and pray for all that will be.

You could use these words: 'For all that has been, thanks; for all that will be, yes' (Dag Hammarskjöld).

Voice We are God's people, built together as one, Jesus himself is our cornerstone. We are citizens with the saints, Building on all that has gone before. Amen.

Blessing

Minister May the peace of God be in this place (*stretch hands out into the building*).
May the peace of God be in our homes (*stretch hands out towards doors and windows*).
May the peace of God be in or hearts (*place hands over own body*).
And the blessing of God,
Father, Son and Holy Spirit,
be with us all, this day and always.

All **Amen.**

The dismissal

Minister Like living stones, go in peace to proclaim the mighty acts of God.

All **Thanks be to God.**

A mini-drama based on Genesis 28.10–22

You will need a narrator, and two people to play God and Jacob (Jacob could wear a simple headdress), and something to represent the stone.

(Jacob walks to the front, and then lies down on stone. Narrator reads from lectern. God moves to stand next to sleeping figure to read.)

Narrator   Jacob was travelling late at night, too late to go any further. So he lay down, using a stone as a pillow, and he fell fast asleep, and as he slept he dreamt.

He saw a ladder, an incredible ladder, a ladder that reached from earth to heaven. On the rungs of the ladder were angels, moving up to heaven, moving down to earth.

Then God came and stood by Jacob.

God   I am the Lord, the God of Abraham and Sarah, Isaac and Rebekah. This land where you are sleeping is yours. Your children and their children and theirs and theirs and theirs will spread to the east, the south, the north, the west. All the earth will be blessed through them. I am with you, I will keep you wherever you go. I will not leave you.

(God moves away.)

Narrator   Jacob woke up.

Jacob   Surely this is a special place. God is here – and I didn't know! This is the house of God and the gate of heaven!

Narrator   So Jacob took the stone that he had slept on and set it upright. He poured oil over it.

Jacob   I am calling this place Bethel, for it is the house of God. And I promise that if God keeps me and feeds me and looks after me, this place will be God's house.

Festivals Together (London: SPCK). Copyright © Sandra Millar 2012

Biblical and other resources

Astley, Neil (ed.), *Being Alive*, Tarset: Bloodaxe, 2004.

Barfield, Maggie, *The Big Bible Story Book: 188 Bible Stories to Enjoy Together*, Bletchley: Scripture Union, 2007.

Book of Common Prayer.

Common Worship: Additional Collects, London: Church House Publishing, 2004.

Common Worship: Times and Seasons, London: Church House Publishing, 2006.

Common Worship: Services and Prayers for the Church of England, London: Church House Publishing, 2000.

Complete Anglican Hymns Old and New, Stowmarket: Kevin Mayhew, 1976.

Dainty, Peter, *The Electric Bible: Poems for Public Worship*, Stowmarket: Kevin Mayhew, 2003.

Dennis, Trevor, *The Book of Books*, Oxford: Lion Hudson, 2009.

Experience Easter, Gloucester: Jumping Fish, 2007.

Guinness, Michele (ed.), *Tapestry of Voices: Meditations in Celebration of Women*, London: Triangle, 1993.

Hartman, Bob and Krisztina Kallai Nagy, *The Lion Storyteller Bible*, Oxford: Lion Hudson, 2008.

Millar, Sandra, *Resourcing Easter*, Gloucester: Jumping Fish, 2008.

Millar, Sandra, *Resourcing November*, Gloucester: Jumping Fish, 2009.

New Patterns for Worship, London: Church House Publishing, 2008.

Peterson, Eugene H., *The Message*, Colorado Springs, CO: NavPress Publishing Group, 1993.

The St Hilda Community, *New Women Included: A Book of Services and Prayers*, London: SPCK, 1996.